STOCK-CAR RACING LIVES

STOCK-CAR RACING LIVES

BY RICHARD SOWERS

PHOTOGRAPHY BY NIGEL KINRADE

DESIGN BY TOM MORGAN

 DAVID BULL PUBLISHING

CONTENTS

Library of Congress Cataloging-in-Publication:
Sowers, Richard, 1950-
    Stock-car racing lives / by Richard Sowers ; photographs by Nigel Kinrade.
        p. cm
    ISBN 1-893618-14-5 (softcover)
    1. Automobile racing drivers—United States—Biography. 2. Stock car racing—
United States. I. Title.

GV1032.A1 S63 2000
796.72'092'273—dc21
[B]
                                                                00-057978

David Bull Publishing, logo, and colophon are trademarks of David Bull Publishing, Inc.

Book design: Blue Design, Portland, Maine (www.bluedes.com)

Printed in Hong Kong

10 9 8 7 6 5 4 3 2 1

David Bull Publishing
4250 East Camelback Road
Suite K150
Phoenix, AZ 85018

602-852-9500
602-852-9503 (fax)

www.bullpublishing.com

Page 2: Buckshot Jones admits he struggled through his 1999
campaign as a Winston Cup rookie, comparing the experience to
"going back to school." He failed to qualify eight times.

Pages 4 and 5: T. Taylor Warren probably has taken more than
1,000,000 motorsports photographs during his career. From this
unique perspective, he has seen firsthand the dramatic growth in
NASCAR and the changes it has brought.

Page 6: While he has spent years supervising the world's fastest stock
cars as they thunder down pit road, NASCAR official Jimmy Cox often
prefers to travel by motorcycle.

Opposite: Almost everyone in the garage has to look up to Big John
Youk, who is a gas man and cook for Team SABCO. At 6 feet 6 and
292 pounds, he is an imposing figure.

Pages 10 and 11: Seen from behind, QVC's temporary set in Las Vegas
dwarfs host Dan Hughes and Mark Martin, who are on the left. The two
cameramen and video monitors can be seen in the center with the
studio audience behind in the stands. Telephones wired direct to West
Chester, Pa., allow the studio audience to buy items at the same time
the home audience sees them.

PREFACE

When 43 cars thunder toward the start/finish line at the outset of a NASCAR Winston Cup race, they become the focus of some 190,000 people in the grandstands, 10 million TV viewers, and a couple of million radio listeners.

While the 43 men driving those machines are in the spotlight, as many as 14,000 people have worked behind the scenes to make that race a reality.

Many have spent months of preparation to help give fans of America's fastest-growing sport a Sunday afternoon or Saturday night of thrills and excitement, yet don't even have a chance to see the race themselves. Their race-day duties simply don't include a view of the track.

Stock-Car Racing Lives presents the stories of people who devote their lives to the sport. Some are relative newcomers, others grizzled veterans. You'll learn that 80-hour work weeks— or more—are not uncommon. And that's true not only for those who own, build, and drive the cars, but for those who sell the tickets and souvenirs, feed the fans, maintain the facilities, officiate the races, and the media who chronicle the sport. It's even true for sponsors, wives, ministers, and others who labor behind the scenes.

As acclaimed motorsports artist Sam Bass says: "Most people work during the week and go home on weekends. NASCAR people work during the week and go away on weekends to work. You've got to have a lot of love for what you're doing to do that."

Opposite: **After Dale Jarrett earned his third Daytona 500 victory in February of 2000, he received a congratulatory hug from his father, Ned.**

Stock-Car Racing Lives tells the stories of both world-famous figures and those with whom you might not be familiar, yet have played significant roles in the sport's evolution from well-kept Southern secret to the mainstream of American culture.

Stock-Car Racing Lives takes you behind the scenes to learn what those men and women consider the most significant changes in that evolution. You'll also learn about their duties, highlights, concerns, opinions—even their diets—and what drew them to the sport. And you'll see how—or if—people involved in the sport find time for a personal life amid the pressure and dedication it takes to live *Stock-Car Racing Lives*.

JAY ADAMCZYK
Webmaster, Jayski.com

When former graphic artist and disk jockey Jay Adamczyk began devoting his free time to a stock-car racing Internet site, his friends thought he was nuts. "But now they see it's a business that's pretty popular," he says.

In fact, the Winston Cup Series may be the only circuit in motorsports that can boast that its average attendance exceeds the number of fans who inspect Adamczyk's creation—www.Jayski.com—every day.

Adamczyk established the site on August 26, 1996. "Lake Speed lost his sponsorship with Spam, and I was having a hard time finding information. So I started a site," he says. "It was just a hobby. When I got my first 100 hits in a day, I thought that was super. [Growth] has been a steady plateau. It's word of mouth. People e-mail and say, 'I love your page. I tell all my NASCAR friends about it.' I had an interview on TNN, and that really helped the hits—about 10,000 more a day. During the season, I get around 55,000 a day, a high of 70,000—pretty wild."

Despite its popularity, Jayski.com remained a hobby until December of 1999, when sponsorship from Racing Champions allowed Adamczyk to quit his job as a computer programmer with the Federal Aviation Administration. "I was basically killing myself. Something had to give," he says. "The site had a few ads, but [revenues] wouldn't even cover a car pay-

Opposite: What began as a hobby for Jay Adamczyk has become www.Jayski.com, one of auto racing's most popular Internet sites.

"I don't want to sound conceited, but it's rare that somebody tells me something I don't already know. My dad will say, 'I just saw this in the paper.' I say, 'Dad, I had it two weeks ago.' I'm not worried about scoops."

ment. With Racing Champions involved, I'm hoping to get close to 100,000 [visitors] a day."

Although Jayski.com often scoops other media outlets, Adamczyk's goal is simply to be the best source of information about NASCAR.

"I don't want to sound conceited, but it's rare that somebody tells me something I don't already know," he says. "My dad will say, 'I just saw this in the paper.' I say, 'Dad, I had it two weeks ago.' I'm not worried about scoops. I've never been a big rumor person. When I hear something that's unconfirmed, I want to be sure other people understand it's rumor. If it's from a good source, I'll post it. But if some Joe Blow I've never heard of e-mails me and says, 'I heard this guy's getting fired,' I won't put that up.

"I check things out. I wait for the official announcement more than I used to. One of the most difficult times was in the '98 season. Rumors floated around about Mike Skinner getting let go from the 31 car. I posted the rumor. I was getting hammered all around—'just another Internet rumor'—and I felt it was directed at me. One thing that really irritates me is hate mail. It takes every fiber of my being not to do anything with it. I can't expect everyone to like me or the site, but it annoys me when they don't. People think I'm always looking for a scoop or a rumor, that I'll post anything—which is *so* extremely untrue. Everything I put up has a link to another site or a source. You get burned, you learn your lesson. I'm just trying to do the job the best I can. I'm not trying to hurt anyone or get anyone fired.

"A ton of sources have come to me. They usually e-mail me. A lot of them won't give their names, but they'll throw me a bone. If it becomes true, I let it build before I post something. Billy Standridge, the first driver to e-mail me, was a big help. Some people think he's small time, but he was a Winston Cup driver and a big name to me. I'll get on a team site, e-mail, and ask, 'I just heard this. Is it true?' I'll build sources that way. Now, I get a lot of press releases. P.R. people started finding out about me, and I guess they wanted to quash things before they got out there."

Although Adamczyk has had favorite drivers in the past, NASCAR racers should be relieved to learn he no longer does.

"In the early '70s, my dad took me to Indy qualifying at Pocono. That's how I got hooked," he recalls. "I met Mark Donohue, my favorite driver from then until he passed away [in a practice accident]. As a kid, Donohue and [former Phillies shortstop] Larry Bowa were my idols. Donohue was real smart, down to earth, and Bowa was a small, scrappy guy. After Donohue, I really didn't follow a driver until Alan Kulwicki. When he got killed, I started following Davey Allison, and he got killed. When Ernie Irvan replaced Allison at Robert Yates Racing, I started following him. Until his [life-threatening] accident, he was *the* driver. When he got hurt, I said, 'I'm not going to have any more favorites.' I was losing them left and right."

Although he has lost his share of favorites, Adamczyk's dedication to Jayski.com should help prevent him from losing his fans.

"People get the impression I don't sleep, that I'm on the phone or computer 24 hours a day. I try to spend time with my dog, the family, friends. I'm 38 and single. I like to read about sports, see movies, watch TV, listen to music."

"I haven't missed a day of updating the site in two years. Even when I went to Italy, I had my laptop with me," he says. "I get up around 7 and turn on my computer. While it's warming up, I feed my dog and two cats. I check my e-mail. I get 150 or 200 messages a day. If I have an abnormal amount, I know something's going on. Then I bring up three sites: That's Racing, Speedvision, and NASCAR Online. Then I work on the site. I have it down to a science. I'll probably work until 10, then send the updates out. I try to update kind of haphazardly. I don't want anybody to have a pattern of what I'm doing. Around noon, I'll work for a couple hours. During the season at 7 p.m., I'm watching *RPM 2Night*. After dinner, I'll work a couple hours. I try to send an update around midnight, then call it a day.

"People think I go to races all the time. You're going to be amazed at this: I go to one race a year—at Dover—and it freaks me out. I don't like crowds.

"People get the impression I don't sleep, that I'm on the phone or computer 24 hours a day. I try to spend time with my dog, the family, friends. I'm 38 and single. I like to read about sports, see movies, watch TV, listen to music."

When the site's popularity exceeded expectations, Adamczyk, in an effort to maintain his privacy, deleted personal information, which subsequently led to considerable speculation about Jayski's identity.

"When I started getting a little notoriety, I mentioned on the page I was going to Dover and wouldn't be updating," he says. "I got 100 e-mails from people wanting to meet me. I thought, 'This is too much!' I get interview requests and say, 'Do I really want to do this?' It's nice to be able to go to a store and nobody knows who I am. I can't imagine what Jeff Gordon and Dale Earnhardt go through."

Those seeking Jayski's identity should have checked with his old military buddies. "Jayski is my nickname I got in the Air Force," he says. "My instructor couldn't say my Polish name. He kept calling me Adamski. Then he said, 'I'm going to call you Jayski,' and it stuck."

One of the highlights for Adamczyk—The Nashville Network feature in which his face was blurred beyond recognition—also contributed to the mystery.

"Randy Pemberton and two cameramen—three of the nicest guys I've ever met—came to the house. Obscuring my face was Randy's choice. I said, 'I don't care if you blur it or not.' You could see my hat and the bottom of my goatee," he says. "They treated me like I was a celebrity, which I don't see myself as—just a guy on the Internet. After the interview was televised, Ned Jarrett, Steve Waid, and Stephanie Durner—people I respect—had good things to say about the site. The other thing I felt was pretty big was [*Charlotte Observer* motorsports reporter] David Poole ranking me the 25th most influential person in NASCAR. My sister gave me the article for Christmas in a frame."

Despite being racing's uncrowned king of the internet, Adamczyk thinks the best development in the sport is the wealth of information now available via another medium.

"I remember watching *Wide World of Sports* when I was a kid, happy just to see five minutes of Richard Petty winning a race," he recalls. "Now, you have *RPM 2 Night*, *RaceDay*, *Inside NASCAR*, *Inside Winston Cup Racing*, Speedvision. You've got qualifying on TV, which is awesome. The TV coverage is unbelievable."

Considering he was selected one of the 25 most influential people in NASCAR six months before he turned his hobby into a profession, Adamczyk is more concerned that his computer will crash than his career.

"One of the most difficult things is server problems, because it's beyond my control," he says. "That doesn't happen much now because of improvements in technology and equipment. But when I started, that was frustrating.

"I like working on the computer. I enjoy racing, Winston Cup especially. When I'm involved in something, I like knowing everything I can about it. This keeps me abreast of everything. I like being my own boss. But if Racing Champions said, 'We can't work with you,' I'd look for a job. My last three jobs, I could go back to in a heartbeat. I'm more worried about where the next news bite's coming from."

Sam Bass
Motorsports Artist

"I know how fortunate I am to have a career doing something I love," Sam Bass says. "This is my hobby, my love. Give me a list of all careers. This is it for me. I love drawing and painting, but what I *really* love to draw and paint are race cars and the people who drive them."

As owner of Sam Bass Illustration & Design, Inc., in Concord, N.C., the Hopewell, Va., native reinforces that love by painting some 50 originals a year and designing the color schemes of nearly two dozen cars that compete in the Winston Cup or Busch Series.

"I was six or seven when I went to my first race at Southside Speedway in Richmond,' Bass says. "I was mesmerized by the color, the speed, the crowd reaction. I was given a program that night and saw the drawing on the front, and I *knew* at that point in my life I wanted to be part of racing.

"This sport is about getting an opportunity and making the most of it. It's meeting this person, getting authorization to do a painting. I was a charter member of the Bobby Allison Fan Club in the early '70s. In 1981, my first year at Virginia Commonwealth University, I went to a fan club banquet to present him with a painting I'd done, and he was beaming from ear to ear. That August, I went to Talladega and stood at the garage gate for several hours, waiting to get a painting of his car autographed. While Bobby and his crew were signing the painting, people said, 'Did you do this?' Seeing the reaction to that painting blew my mind. I picked up three commissions that weekend. I thought, 'If I could string enough of these together, *maybe* I could live my dream of working in this full time. This would be a really cool career.'

"Later that fall, I drove to Richmond Fairgrounds Raceway to meet [President] Paul Sawyer. I was a nervous wreck. I carried a bunch of drawings and said, 'I would really like to get a garage pass.' I think he really sensed my desire. He gave me my first garage pass, and that snowballed into other things. In late 1984, Charlotte Motor Speedway said, 'We want you to do our program cover,' and I've done every one since. Humpy Wheeler and Tom Cotter gave me opportunities with Char-

> **Below:** When it comes to doing business, the garage area is where the rubber meets the road. During race weekends Sam Bass has impromptu discussions with corporate clients and drivers as well as planned events to introduce paint schemes. This is Daytona in February 2000.

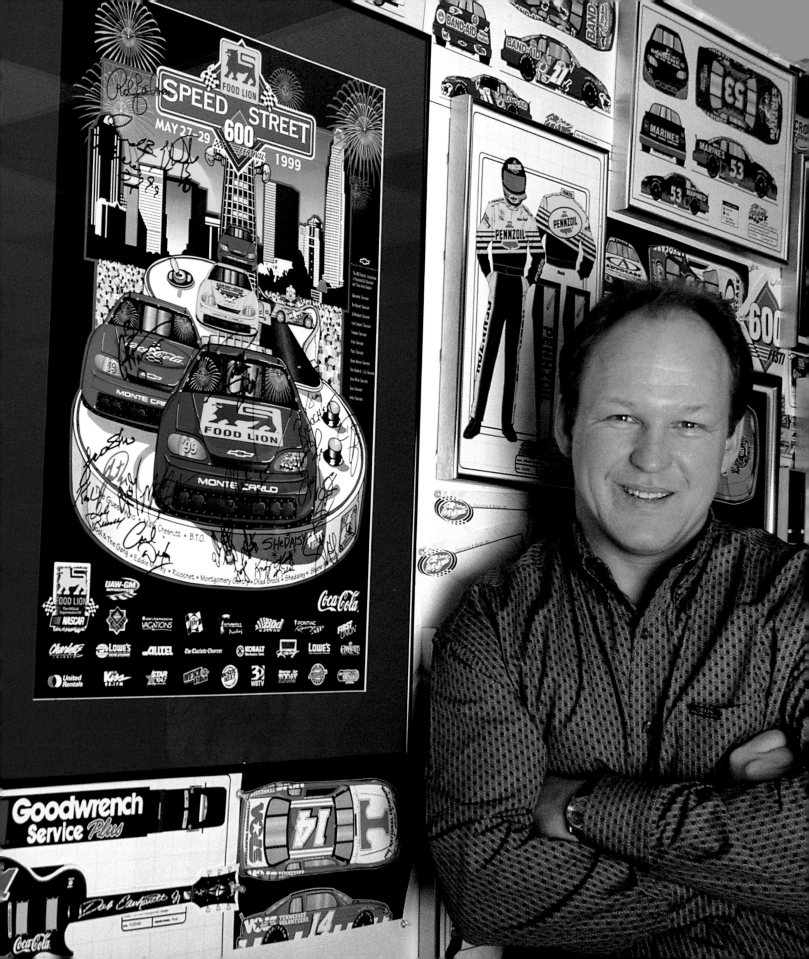

lotte. Humpy is a creative genius. He's always thinking, never satisfied with the status quo.

"One of the first drivers I got a chance to do artwork for was Dale Earnhardt in the mid-'80s. Dale has been the single biggest supporter of my artwork since. He has been incredible. Being able to say, 'Dale Earnhardt is on a Wheaties box, and Sam Bass illustrated it,' was an awesome feeling.

"For six years, it was bits and pieces. I worked in the procurement department at a military base. In 1987, Miller Brewing Company had me design the Bobby Allison race car for 1988. That was the impetus to say, 'I'm making the plunge.' Then, Bobby asked if I'd design his Busch car. So I designed a car for Piper Aircraft and the Miller car. I went to Daytona and saw him win with the Busch car and win the Daytona 500 in paint schemes

Opposite: **From his studio near Lowe's Motor Speedway in Concord, N.C., Bass produces about 50 original paintings per year that depict Winston Cup racing. He also designs team uniforms and paint schemes for race cars and haulers.**

that had *never* been run before. That was one of my best moments. The other was at the 1993 Unocal dinner at Charlotte Motor Speedway. They were awarding Davey Allison a painting for winning the previous year's Coca-Cola 600. Humpy said, 'I want something that will really get to Davey.' I had Bobby's car reflecting underneath Davey's in the pavement, Davey holding the 600 trophy and, over his shoulder, Bobby years earlier winning the 600 and holding his trophy. I was in the audience, and Davey looked right in my eyes and said, 'Sam, this is *awesome*.' It was an amazing feeling, but later it meant even more. *The* worst day of my career was when I heard Davey had been killed in a helicopter crash.

"A lot of people stop by to see my artwork," Bass adds. "I might be having the worst day. But when I meet them, that 30 seconds or five minutes or 10 minutes they spend with me is all they've got to judge me. My worries and frustrations are irrelevant. It's my job to show them the appreciation I have for them and make them feel they've had a great experience here.

"I'm sincere in what I'm doing. This sport means a *whole* lot to me. I'm in this for the long run, not the quick dollar. If you go, 'I want to do this for X dollars,' you lose focus. I feel if you treat your clients right, the money takes care of itself. There has never been a client who said, 'We're not happy with what you're doing.' That's very important to me. I want my clients to like my artwork. But it's far more important they like me and know what's behind that artwork.

"The other part of my business, the design work, I used to render a car by hand. Now, I do it with computers. Television has affected the design business. Look at photos up to 1984 or '85. Nobody cared how big their logo was on the hood. We started getting increased TV coverage, and logos went from whatever the size was to: 'We've got to have a six-foot-by-eight-foot logo on that hood!'

"The whole creative spirit of what I do is a joy. In a lot of degrees, my mother has been my mentor. She's kind of a Martha Stewart-like person. I see exactly where I got my creativity. I had an art instructor in high school, Matt Smart, who had so much enthusiasm and talent that

I aspired to be like him. A college instructor, Barbara Tisseratt, was very supportive of me to pursue my dream, what I wanted to paint—even if it was stock cars.

"To be creative is a challenge. To be creative in eight hours is a bigger challenge. The deadlines, the anxiety, the fear, make it tough. When you've got to design a race car, that's fun. When you've got to design a race car that meets all the criteria your client gives you and do it in a specific amount of time, it's serious business.

"I always want to see something in my latest work that's an improvement over what I did the last time. There's a fine line between being too critical and not being critical enough. I think not to be 100 percent happy with anything you do is healthy, because it's going to keep you working harder and trying to improve.

"My typical day is about seven in the morning to nine or 10 at night. Between September and February, when you're announcing sponsorships, creating new paint schemes, and putting together all the parts and pieces P.R. firms and race teams need, it's about 18 hours a day seven days a week. People say, 'That must be dreadful.' But an 18-hour day for me is like an eight-hour day for people who don't like what they're doing. People ask, 'What's the average time to do a painting?' I say, 'Eighty hours.' To the average person, 80 hours is two work weeks. To me, it might be a three-day weekend. Some of my best work has come on a three-day weekend, because you're so focused. There's nothing in your life but that painting.

"My personal life is not what I ultimately want it to be. I'm married to a godsend as far as my schedule is concerned. My wife, Denise, runs the business. I eat at my desk. I'm diabetic, but not as disciplined as I should be. If you're getting ready to make a peanut butter bagel and Dale and Teresa Earnhardt show up, you're going to talk with them about their project. That's taking care of your client. I have a lot of clients who feel like they're my only client, and that's *exactly* the way they

should feel. I had a client call the other day and say, 'I just wanted to tell you we loved what you did.' As far as I'm concerned, they don't even have to send a paycheck. That was the ultimate.

"I want to document the sport," he adds. "I look forward to the 75th anniversary of NASCAR and, hopefully, will be around for the 100th. Picasso and a lot of artists were painting in their eighties and nineties. I see myself doing that. I admire Picasso because of his creative spirit and how many different styles he had during his career. I really admire LeRoy Neiman because he can go to any major event and be recognized as a great artist in that field. That's *phenomenal*.

"I obviously want to be recognized as a good artist in NASCAR. Fortunately, race fans probably are more familiar with what I'm doing than Picasso. I would *never* be able to hold a brush to Pablo Picasso, but at the end of my career, if vast contingencies of fans say, 'He was the guy in NASCAR,' that would be cool."

Opposite: Bass poses with Wyatt Wells outside Lowe's Motor Speedway's Media Center in October 1999. Wells, a first grader from Minnesota, won a Revell-sponsored national design contest and worked with Bass, who was a judge, to complete his winning car design.

TIM BERTONI/DAN HUGHES
QVC's *For Race Fans Only*

"I was working for a company in Delaware in 1990 that was making bronze ingots for Hallmark stores," recalls Tim Bertoni. "George deBidart, who now has a Busch team, said, 'Have you thought of putting NASCAR drivers on these? This would be a great collectible.' We went to see Richard Petty, Harry Gant, Rusty Wallace, and Geoff Bodine, and licensed the ingots.

"I said, 'I'm taking them to QVC.' I met with the collectible buyer and said, 'We want to do this Petty item.' She said to get more Petty items—and Petty himself. George and I went back to North Carolina, pulled together about 12 Petty items, got Richard, and ended up doing our show."

That was the unlikely birth of QVC's popular *For Race Fans Only*, the braintrust of host Dan Hughes and Bertoni, now Vice President of Electronic Retail Marketing for The Source International, QVC's on-site motorsports production team.

"Television is the reason for why the sport and drivers have become so popular," Bertoni says. "The show is a unique marketing opportunity. There are fans who've never been to a race. They watch it on TV. We get calls from Alaska, Hawaii. They had no way of getting Dale Earnhardt merchandise. Now, they do. It's a huge business. Everybody thought there was no way we could do the numbers we did during the 50th anniversary year, but we're ahead. It's amazing."

So is the success of *For Race Fans Only*, a unique blend of souvenir sales and driver interviews.

"We've done shows at 1 in the morning that have been hugely successful," Hughes says. "There are so many new people watching this sport. Those people become our customers and loyal followers. A lot of credit would go to the biggest names in the sport. Dale Earnhardt has probably done more live TV at QVC than anywhere. I sit down with him for sometimes three hours, and it becomes a lot more than talking about collectibles. It's talking about Dale."

"Hard-core fans are religious watchers," Bertoni says. "If they've seen 15 or 20 interviews with Dale and are willing to sit there and buy the stuff, they want to hear different, unique

Opposite: From the $10 million mobile production studio, Tim Bertoni monitors orders in West Chester, Pa., and keeps Dan Hughes apprised of when they are selling out of items. The production team in front of the control board determines what the home audience sees.

things. To keep the show fresh is a tremendous challenge.

"If every show was 100 percent diecast or apparel, it would get boring. The last show with Dale, we were selling everything from Earnhardt robes to mailboxes. I'm already looking for products for next year. I'm traveling a week out of a month, meeting with manufacturers and product developers. You try to put yourself in the consumer's position and make intelligent buying decisions. But you've got to be on the cutting edge. Most of the products we do are national launches.

"The most difficult part is booking drivers. I drive drivers and agents crazy. The Dale Earnhardts and Jeff Gordons of the world are being pulled in a million directions. We've gotten very creative about getting them. They'll say Jeff's not available on the 15th. I'll say, 'What if we do it on the 16th or 17th? Tell me when he's available, and we'll change our schedule.' We're doing more shows from tracks because it's difficult to get drivers to come to West Chester (Pa.). We have a $10 million production facility that travels all over the country. QVC is willing to go that extra mile to make these shows happen.

"Quality, Value, and Convenience is about giving the customer a quality product in a convenient way. It's easy to do, but difficult to do successfully. You've got to have great product and a host who has credibility."

That's Hughes, who calls his role "a passion that's just incredible."

"If somebody had told me my days would be like this 10 years ago when I went to work at QVC," Hughes said, "I'd have said, 'Why would I want to do *that*?' I co-host a show Monday through Friday from 7 to 9 a.m. I'm up at 3, in the studio between 4:30 and 5. I get home around 2 in the afternoon. When I'm on the road, it's work. I order room service. I'm digging for those one or two questions where the driver is thinking, 'How did he know that?' I read everything that comes down the pike. With the sport growing as quickly as it has, it gives me a lot more sources of information—web sites, more *good* racing publications. The downside is you're spending a *lot* more time. It takes between 20 and 60 hours of prep for every race show."

"Dan and I spend three to four hours on show day talking about product, about drivers," Bertoni says. "He makes it look easy on camera."

Opposite top: This is how the same Las Vegas set (shown on pages 10-11) appears to QVC's home viewing audience. The headsets allow Hughes and Mark Martin to speak to viewers who call in to chat. Opposite bottom: After finishing a remote telecast from the Action Performance headquarters in Phoenix, Hughes signs autographs for members of the audience.

"My job is to interview," Hughes says. "I also have to sell. To mix the two together isn't easy. Whether I sell $1 billion or $10 worth does not effect my financial outcome. I do not work on commission. What I think of a product shouldn't make one iota of difference. But I'm human. If I really like it, you're going to know.

"The toughest thing is trying to keep the show fresh, keep the interview entertaining and

different. We're able to show there's a human being who happens to be a race driver as opposed to just the hero. I don't want to do anything that hurts them. We're not *Hard Copy.* I spent seven-and-a-half years doing standup comedy. I enjoy laughing and joking with people. We use a soft approach, and we're blessed it works. Most of the drivers are excruciatingly honest about themselves on the air. You can't do two hours of live television and not let the real you come out.

"When we finish the show and Dale Earnhardt, Rusty Wallace, Jeff Gordon, Rick Mast, or Dave Marcis, one of the greatest guys in the world, looks you in the eye and says, 'You do a good job,' that makes it worthwhile."

Hughes has been a race fan since he was eight, when he saw Mario Andretti win the 1969 Indianapolis 500 in his hometown. Yet he and Bertoni rarely see races in person.

"When I'm on the road, it's non-stop work," Bertoni says. "A lot of times, we're eating at Steak N Shake at midnight. I love being home and watching races with my kids, Rachel, Hayley, and Joey. I admire the way my wife, Barbara, balances our life."

"The career path I chose had a lot to do with my marriage not working," Hughes said. "But it was the way I handled it. The man who gives me my paycheck is going to get 110 percent. I didn't give 100 percent at home. That balance is finally there, but it took getting to a certain level of success to realize what I really wanted wasn't monetary. My 14-year-old daughter, Allison, who lives with me, means everything to me. I learn more from her than she learns from me. An example of Allison being a mentor: We had a kitten get out of the house and climb a tree in the yard. Allison, who was three then, said, 'Don't worry. The cat'll come down. Have you ever seen a cat skeleton up in a tree?' I admire individuals who take something everybody else sees and find a different way of looking at it—inventors, comedians, kids."

Hughes wishes viewers had seen a different ending to the show on February 14, 1994.

"We've got a live show with Earnhardt," he recalls. "Because of logistics, I couldn't get to Daytona, and he couldn't get to West Chester. We worked out a simulcast with Channel 2 in Daytona. Dale is in the studio there. I'm home. I close by saying, 'Dale, we appreciate you taking time to be part of the program. Good luck at Daytona, and good night.' Then I thought, 'Wait a minute. It's Valentine's Day.'

"I said, 'We've been plugging your sponsors all night. Don't you want to plug your wife?' On the air! I was shooting for a Valentine's Day opportunity for Dale to say hello to his wife. I thought, 'If Dale doesn't kill me, Teresa will.' There's a painfully long pause. Dale said something to the effect of, 'Teresa, I love you. I'll see you soon.' I saw my career going down in flames. I called the studio in Daytona, and Don Hawk [Earnhardt's business manager] picked up the phone. I said, 'I did not mean to say it that way.' He said, 'Dale won't talk to you.'

"Then I hear Dale laughing in the background."

Opposite: **Bertoni is on the set before the start of a remote telecast of QVC's *For Race Fans Only* from Las Vegas in March 2000. Bertoni oversees all aspects of the show, including planning the guests and selecting the products.**

BRETT BODINE
Winston Cup Owner/Driver

Brett Bodine, who drives for the Winston Cup team he owns with his wife, Diane, readily admits that being a driver/owner has been a struggle.

"It's a matter of funding," he says. "If we had been funded correctly from the start, we wouldn't be in the position we're in. We wouldn't be as far from being competitive as we are, and we wouldn't be in the debt that we're in because of the sponsorship situations that went bad. I don't feel we did anything *wrong* to get ourselves in this position. It just happened."

Bodine purchased his team from the legendary Junior Johnson, for whom he had been driving, when the latter sold his racing interests after the 1995 season.

"I was inspired by [the late] Alan Kulwicki's success," Bodine says of the driver who won the 1992 Winston Cup title as the owner of his team. "We became car owners because racing is our life. We didn't get into it because we thought we could make twice as much money than we could with me just being a driver. The disadvantage of being an owner/driver is that an owner/driver tends to be a racer. His heart is in the competitive side, not the business side. It tends to make him more cognizant of his performance and not the marketing, and sometimes in our sport, sponsorship is driven more by marketing.

"When we purchased the team from Junior, we had one season sponsored by Lowe's. After that year, Lowe's went to another race team and left us unsponsored. There's a lot of interest in our sport, but there isn't as much as one would think from companies that want to hand you $5 million to put their name on the side of a car. And it's hard to make that sales pitch, get your point across, and convince a company to do that. We worked very hard to find a sponsor and got one for '97, Catalyst Communications. It looked really good for us, a three-year deal, very competitive money. Unfortunately, Catalyst didn't pay its bills. In an effort to keep the race team going, Diane and I virtually put ourselves in financial ruin. It ruined us competitively. We're still recovering from it, because we got behind in technology and quality of equipment, and our growth curve was severely stunted because we were so underfunded. We've come through some really hard times to stay in this business as car owners."

Opposite: Brett is one of three Bodine brothers who have competed in Winston Cup racing, along with older brother Geoff and younger brother Todd. Like Brett, Geoff raced for Junior Johnson and had four wins in 1990 and '91.

Late in the 1999 season, primarily in an effort to rid themselves of debt, the Bodines announced they were selling the team to Richard Hilton. But that deal fell through.

"He couldn't get his financing together, but the good news is that we got a sponsor out of it," Bodine says, referring to Ralph's, one of the nation's largest grocery chains. "We're no longer actively trying to sell the team."

Bodine thinks his team eventually can be competitive because of what he considers the most important development in Winston Cup racing since he joined the circuit in 1987. "NASCAR's rules have created the most level playing field we've ever seen," he says.

The primary drawback, however, could be what he considers the worst trend.

"The worst change is the advantage multiple-car teams have over single-car teams because of testing rules and the perception of sponsors that they have to be involved with multiple-car teams to be successful," he says. "And that's not true. You can be a very successful single-car team given the funding. Winston Cup drivers are all champions from somewhere and have won a lot of races somewhere. The biggest misconception is that we don't run hard every lap. I run every lap as hard as that car will go. I *guarantee* most guys running from 30th back are driving just as hard, if not harder, than guys running from 10th forward. Their cars just aren't working as well."

Since Bodine's parents owned and operated Chemung Speedrome in upstate New York for nearly 30 years, it was natural that Brett, younger brother Todd, and older brother Geoff, whose 18 Winston Cup victories include the 1986 Daytona 500, gravitated toward racing.

"In my teens, I told my parents, 'I don't want to own this track. I want to be a driver,'" says Brett, who abandoned his high school basketball and golf careers. "You're only a high school senior once, and I took that year away from being a teenager. In order to race, I worked at a Chevrolet dealership from 3 in the afternoon until 9 at night as an undercoater.

"I was a dean's list student at the State University of New York at Alfred. My senior year at Alfred, I applied at the Rochester Institute of Technology, Wentworth Institute in Boston, and the Massachusetts Institute of Technology. I got accepted at all three. But my plan was to

"The biggest misconception is that we don't run hard every lap. I guarantee most guys running from 30th back are driving just as hard, if not harder, than guys running from 10th forward. Their cars just aren't working as well."

give myself five years, and if I did not meet my criteria for where I thought my driving career should be—winning races in the modified division in the Northeast—then I'd go back to school and get my master's in engineering.

"Through college, I'd go home on weekends and build cars for people to support my part-time racing. My senior year at Alfred, 1979, I went to Dushore, Pennsylvania, over Christmas break. Wayne Miller and I built a NASCAR modified car in three weeks. In the spring of '79, we went to the 250-lap race at Martinsville to compete against the hottest, toughest modifieds in the country—Jerry Cook, Richie Evans, Maynard Troyer, Bugs Stevens, Ken Bouchard, Satch Worley. We started 40th, ended up ninth, and were very proud.

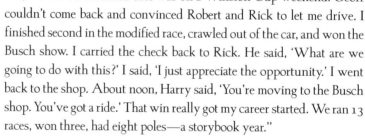

Below: Bodine steps forward to acknowledge the fans' applause during the driver introductions before the April 1999 race at Martinsville. Paychex, a payroll services company, was Bodine's sponsor in 1998 and '99.

"A year later, I married Diane. We struggled trying to scrape a living together running modifieds. I worked in the winter as a welder. She babysat. Diane always believed in my abilities. When she said, 'For better, for worse,' she knew she was getting the 'worse' first. It was tough to live in a mobile home making $125 a week as a race driver. Finally, in 1984, we won what I considered the most prestigious track championship, at Stafford (Conn.) Motor Speedway. Geoff, who was driving for Rick Hendrick, talked [crew chief] Harry Hyde into giving me a job as a fabricator."

Billy Carazzo and Clyde McCloud, for whom Brett had driven in the Northeast, enlisted him to drive their modified car in Martinsville's 250-lapper in the spring of 1985.

"Geoff was going to run the Levi Garrett Busch car for Robert Gee and Rick," Brett recalls. "The race got rained out, and the rescheduled date was on a Winston Cup weekend. Geoff

couldn't come back and convinced Robert and Rick to let me drive. I finished second in the modified race, crawled out of the car, and won the Busch show. I carried the check back to Rick. He said, 'What are we going to do with this?' I said, 'I just appreciate the opportunity.' I went back to the shop. About noon, Harry said, 'You're moving to the Busch shop. You've got a ride.' That win really got my career started. We ran 13 races, won three, had eight poles—a storybook year."

A year later, Bodine earned two more victories, lost the Busch title by 20 points, then moved to Winston Cup.

"I love the competition. The best moment was the 1990 win at North Wilkesboro," says Bodine, who also has five Winston Cup poles. "When you win at the top level, that's pretty exciting. To have everybody there— Dad, Mom, in-laws—to share it was important."

Brett's controversial wreck with Geoff, when they were dueling for the lead in the 1994 Brickyard 400 in which Brett finished second, was

"I love the competition. The best moment was the 1990 win at North Wilkesboro. When you win at the top level, that's pretty exciting. To have everybody there— Dad, Mom, in-laws—to share it was important."

not his nadir. "I was upset over the accusations he made—that the problems we were having away from the track were taken onto the track," Brett says. "We were handling it correctly— out of the public eye. For him to say what he did hurt me. My worst moment was when I lost my best friend, Davey Allison. We had a lot of unfinished things to do together."

Brett says the lack of "time to get everything done I wish I could makes my job difficult. It's not 8-to-5. It's whatever it takes. Our crew guys go three weeks at a time seven days a week. If I take time off, I feel guilty. We don't have what most people consider a normal life. There are times I say, 'Why don't we move to some deserted island and become bums?' "

Bodine was among the last drivers to purchase a motorhome, which helps him balance family and career.

"Motorhomes have been *tremendous* for our sport, a lifesaver to a lot of families," he says. "My daughter, Heidi, travels with us a lot. From the time practice is over until the next morning, we can have *somewhat* of a normal evening, maybe cook out. On the road, we don't usually have free time, but if we're on the West Coast, we might go to Las Vegas for a day. If Diane and I get two or three days, we go to our condo at Daytona Beach. I love sports. Diane says if it's ping pong on TV, I'll watch. If I get a free day, I play golf, but usually I can't unless it's some charity tournament."

Bodine would have considerably more free time if he wasn't a staple at charity functions.

"There's no question our time is more limited than when I got into Winston Cup racing," he says, "but I love that we can do charity work. We can do a lot of things to try to influence kids to do the right thing and to show them that hard work and dedication do pay off. I admire Kyle Petty and Dale Jarrett, because they're very successful and have high-profile sponsors, but still continue to do things that are right for our sport. I hope the guys coming in recognize that's a very important part of their job—to continue the standards guys like Richard Petty and Bobby Allison set. Arnold Palmer, Richard, and Joe DiMaggio were probably the most successful of their time in their sports, and they were good people who did things right and treated other people right—admirable qualities."

DAVID CARMICHAEL
Wheel Cleaner

David Carmichael says he has "always been the type that, if I want something, I'll work hard and get it."

Carmichael decided in 1994 that he wanted to work in Winston Cup racing. So he created a business—polishing the wheels on virtually every transporter and motorhome that race teams, drivers, and officials bring to the track.

"When my wife passed away in Colorado, I couldn't stay," says Carmichael, 44. "I have a brother in Mebane, North Carolina, so I moved my daughters [ages 19 and 13] there. I go see them as often as I can.

Opposite: On an average day, David Carmichael can get 20 wheels this polished and spotless—and even more than that when there is extra daylight in the summer. He follows the circuit from race to race and lives in his van.

"Somehow, I was going to work in racing. I ran a custom motorcycle shop for 15 years, but I'd had enough. In '94, I was standing outside Charlotte Motor Speedway looking at souvenir rigs. Nobody would give me a job. So I asked one guy if I could polish his wheels, and he said, 'Sure.' I polished them, and it snowballed. NASCAR asked me to do one of their rigs. [NASCAR official and pace car driver] Buster Auten gave me a chance. I spent two days on their truck—got the wheels like brand-new, to shine like $1 million. I got a NASCAR license, and I've been in the garage ever since. I do NASCAR's trucks, then do the teams' haulers for money. I spend about three days in the drivers' motorhome lot before their rigs show up.

"I say hello to the drivers, but I don't try to carry on conversations. Kyle Petty has told me to come by his house. Rusty Wallace will make sure he says hello.

"I clean about 20 wheels a day. When it stays daylight until 8 o'clock, I can do more. The chemicals I work with blister my fingers. No pain, no gain—I've always lived by that rule. I've always gone after the dirtiest, nastiest jobs nobody else wanted. Come race day, I try to be finished with my work so I can go to pit road and watch the race.

"I live in a '92 Dodge van. About every track has a shower in the garage, and I shower at truck stops. I've pretty much found all the laundromats, all the good restaurants. I eat at a lot of Waffle Houses. You can't beat the price. I've got a TV in my van, a little black and white. I get four or five channels. It depends on where I am how the reception is. I watch TV and go to bed.

"Every day's exciting, but someday I might want to live in the Bahamas or Hawaii. If that opportunity comes, I'm probably going to jump on it."

BILL CONNELL
Track Announcer

"I've had people tell me I can make a turtle and rabbit race the most exciting thing in the world," says Bill Connell, who has spent more than 35 years honing his distinctive style as a motorsports public address announcer. "There are 150,000 to 200,000 fans sitting below you. These people are getting excited. It's a big show, like going to the carnival or county fair for the first time.

"I wanted to be like BOB MONTGOMERY OF THE UNIVERSAL RACING NET-WORK, one of the greatest announcers in racing," Connell roars in an excellent impersonation. "After a 13-month tour of Vietnam with the Navy, I drove to Concord Speedway. John Gaskey didn't have a full-time announcer. I said, 'I'll announce *for nothing*.' I'd never done a race in my life. Mr. Gaskey had a bag of money from the gate receipts—paid me $25. I thought I was rich.

"I did Starlite, 311, Caraway, Asheville, Hickory, Metrolina, Gaston [in North Carolina], Myrtle Beach and Cherokee [in South Carolina], where [promoter] Rock Gault used to chew tobacco and dip snuff. Every time he'd talk to me, he spit all over my shirt. I've done a lot of Georgia short tracks. Dr. Jerry Punch and I worked together at Hickory Speedway when he was studying to be a doctor. I helped train Jerry, who went on to bigger things. I *completely* trained Bob Rathburn. He's now doing the Braves, a top baseball and basketball announcer. Rathburn, [longtime Cincinnati Reds announcer] Marty Brennaman, [Performance Racing Network Executive Director and anchor] Doug Rice, and I worked together at WRDX and WSTP in Salisbury (N.C.).

"Back in '67, Richard Howard said, 'I'd like for you to announce for me at Charlotte. I'm going to pay you *$250*.' I had been used to $25 a night. I spent 10 years with MRN, 14 years with the Performance Racing Network. I was doing the track announcing at Char-

> **Opposite: Bill Connell** has been the voice of **Lowe's Motor Speedway** since **1967**, when he was hired by former general manager **Richard Howard. Connell** also has extensive radio experience.

lotte, Atlanta, and Daytona, then rushing out to do the radio, which they'd feed over the P.A. I produced *The Pros in Motorsports* for Fox Sports South, 42 half-hour shows a year, for 14 years. I'm still doing radio talk shows at Daytona and at other tracks, doing track announcing at Las Vegas, Atlanta, and Charlotte.

"We've never lived a normal life. I used to be on the road until 2 or 3 in the morning at a short-track race. My biggest backer would have to be my wife, Sherry. Announcers and other people in this business relied too much on our wives to raise our children while we were trying to make a living. I've got two grown children. I feel bad I missed a lot of great things in our children's lives.

"NASCAR's best improvement is the way they've marketed this program, the promotions and publicity," he adds. "Winston really started the building stage with the millions it put into this series, and television has done wonders for this sport. But one of the greatest improvements is they've got the cars more equal than ever. They're really competitive, and you see a lot better racing than we've ever seen.

"I love calling that side-by-side racing. I'm going to tell it like I see it. If they're a little wild, make it wild. If they're six car lengths apart, make 'em three apart. A little exaggeration never hurt anybody on the race track. Warlords and gladiators, kaleidoscope of colors—all this stuff I've come up with—is exciting.

"It's hard for me, even when I was sick with cancer in 1998, to miss a couple months of racing. The worst moment was when I laid the microphone down in March of 1998 at Atlanta, not knowing if I'd ever announce again. I was one scared big ol' boy going into that operating room. I didn't know when they removed the kidney how my body was going to react. But when I got in that operating room, I had the most tremendous peace come over me before they put me to sleep I've ever had. God gave me strength. The cancer was defeated, I understand, when they took the kidney. I made up my mind I was going to come back. I was back that *May*. We all get old and can be replaced. The day's coming that I'm going to step aside, and somebody else is going to step in. I haven't had the *best* of health since the surgery, but I'm back and thankful."

Connell also is enjoying life on the road more than in the days when he was traveling to short tracks and arriving home in Landis, N.C., around 3 a.m.

"The No. 1 man I have to credit is Humpy Wheeler. He genuinely cares about drivers, his track, his fans. Humpy tells people I'm one of the best track announcers in the business. If I've ever had a mentor who has guided me, it has been Humpy."

"I've never been too busy to eat," he said. "Do I look like it? I'll leave the catered food to go to Atlanta's press box, Jerry Gappens's press box [at Lowe's Motor Speedway], Las Vegas's press box, and Texas's press box, because Jane Hogan is doing the cooking. You eat race-track food 80 percent of the time, but you have a special restaurant everywhere you go. My free time in Las Vegas, I like to pull handles on the dollar machines. I won about $10,000 in 1998. Last year, I hit $13,200 on the Mardi Gras machine. In Atlanta, I sit around the Renaissance [Atlanta Hotel Concourse] and relax. They've got a great pool, good sauna, hot tub. That's what this old body needs.

"The 600 and The Winston is about 10 days solid," Connell adds. "We're there at 5 and 6 in the morning on race days until midnight or 1 or 2 in the morning. Until we drop the checkered flag on the 600, you feel fine. But when that flag comes out, my wife accuses me of being grouchy for two days because you feel like you've got the flu. Your adrenaline's gone, but it was worth every inch of that adrenaline for those 10 days—sometimes 12 hours a day on that microphone—to make sure those fans were excited, to know there was $1 million worth of concession food sold during the big day, to make sure they were happy with what they saw, and that you did your job."

That job has its dark side, however.

"Bad wrecks *really* bring you down, but you can't turn that switch on and be down," Connell says. "You've got to be the same Bill Connell, no matter who was hurt, no matter if it was a fatality. You've got to be professional. That's what makes my job difficult. It's tough when somebody is hurt on the track. What occurred at Lowe's Motor Speedway [when three spectators were killed at an Indy Racing League event in May of 1999] was as tough as anything I've ever faced."

Connell also has endured the loss of most of his favorite drivers.

"I admired Tiny Lund, Tim Flock, and Daryl Dieringer, and I greatly admired Marty Robbins. He was great for this sport. He was so good with the fans. You'd never know he was the big singing star, the millionaire. The No. 1 man I have to credit is [Lowe's Motor Speedway President and General Manager] Humpy Wheeler. He genuinely *cares* about drivers, his track, his fans. Humpy tells people I'm one of the best track announcers in the business. If I've ever had a mentor who has guided me, it has been Humpy. He has been instrumental in the movies I've done—*The Last American Hero, Greased Lightening, Stroker Ace, Hard Driver, Days of Thunder, Stand On It,* and *The James Dean Story.* Riding in the 600 Festival Parade on a float with NASCAR's top drivers and the fans waving and saying, 'Hey, Connell,' and being in the movies with Gary Busey, Jeff Bridges, Richard Pryor, Ned Beatty, Burt Reynolds, and Loni Anderson are the highlights of my career. When you guys put this ol' boy under the ground, I'll always be 18, 20, or 25 on film, and some TV station somewhere will be showing those movies."

RAY COOPER
Chevrolet's Winston Cup Publicist

When fans read the coverage of a Winston Cup event in their newspaper, the writer often has presented the views of a dozen or more drivers about the race. Most fans have never pondered how the writer corralled so many drivers who happened to be spread out over hundreds of acres and in a hurry to leave the premises.

The truth is, without considerable help from friends like Ray Cooper, Chevrolet's Winston Cup publicist since 1989, the quotes from most of those drivers probably wouldn't appear in your morning newspaper.

"I'll bet 75 percent of the drivers' newspaper quotes are from the notes we do," Cooper says. "In the stories on qualifying or a race, the percentage may be even higher."

Cooper has made a science of tracking down Chevrolet drivers after qualifying and races to provide their comments to the media.

"[Dale] Earnhardt always gets out quickly. A few others don't stick around. You want to get them first," he says. "It's tougher now, because their time is more limited. The drivers make it tough sometimes. If they'd just stop for a minute and talk, that'd be it. They might want to talk to CBS or ABC, but when they get through with that, they don't want to talk to anybody else. If they can talk to them for 30 seconds, they can talk to me for 30 seconds. After they talk to me, everybody will have the information. Some of the drivers don't understand that after all these years."

Cooper and his counterparts from other manufacturers and the tracks provide so much information that Cooper says a writer "could sit at home and report on a race if he had the notes and knew anything about it at all. I think some publications do that. I like that. It's job security."

Cooper could have used similar help when he covered his first race, the 1983 Goody's 500 at Martinsville, Va.

Opposite: **Ray Cooper interviews three-time Winston Cup champion and Chevrolet driver Jeff Gordon.**

"I was a copy editor at the *Greensboro News & Record*, and I hated it. I worked every night, 4 p.m. until 1 in the morning, worked every weekend," Cooper recalls. "I was so tired of working at that newspaper every night that I was willing to do anything. They asked for volunteers to do auto racing. I'd never been to one, didn't know what I was doing.

Ricky Rudd won the race. I didn't know Ricky from Adam. Then I went to Charlotte, and that's the race Richard Petty got caught with the big engine and tires on the wrong side. I was there until 11 that night, wrote two stories, and couldn't begin to tell you what I'd written. The guys at Greensboro didn't care for racing, so if I'd had something totally wrong, they wouldn't have known.

"It took me that season plus the next to enjoy racing, but newspaper work is hard. You don't twiddle your thumbs when you're putting out the paper or covering an event. So in 1988, when Bob Moore, who was then with Winston, told me Dave Hedrick, who was with Cadillac, was going to Chevrolet to start a motorsports program, I started calling Hedrick and got the job. I haven't missed a race since. I admire Tom Roberts [publicist for the Miller Lite Ford]. He's one of the few who has been to more consecutive races than I have."

Cooper says alterations in Winston Cup facilities have helped make his job easier—and harder.

"Some of the media centers were like cracker boxes, so upgrading the facilities for the media has been great," he says. "But the worst change has been tracks adding more grandstand seats and not more roads, getting 50,000 more people in there. I hate finishing work three hours after a race and still having to wait to get out.

"I'm usually there pretty late on Fridays and Sundays. Just about every town we go to, there's a favorite restaurant. But sometimes you don't even feel like food. You just want to get away from the track, get a shower, go to bed. Most places, I can't get home on Sunday because most of my work is after the race. I also have Budweiser and Kodak deals, so I have press releases to write for them. I start those on Monday. Winston has a teleconference on Tuesday. If there's a Chevrolet guy on, I'll listen to it. To transcribe an hour's worth might take four. Then you've got to print it, fax it, and e-mail it. That's all day. It's demanding time-wise. Then, Thursday, you're off to the races. California, Phoenix, everything up north, you fly. And that's really a pain.

Opposite top: Cooper and Performance Racing Network radio reporter Steve Richards at work in the garage at Darlington. Opposite bottom: In the media center at Rockingham, Cooper blazes away on his computer, typing his pre-race notes.

"My life was better when I first started this job because I was home three days a week. My wife was a schoolteacher, so I never got to see her when I was working at night. So we saw each other more for about five years. When I was home, I worked a little, but not as much as now. I've been married 20 years, and my wife and I are separated and have two kids. This job is not glamorous. It wears you out."

Then why continue?

"When a writer tells you, 'Good job,' after you've been there all day and cranked out eight or nine pages of notes, that's pretty gratifying. Two years ago, the press guys gave me a golf bag. That was pretty gratifying," he says. "What else can I do and make as much money? Nothing. And I've been a part of it so long, it's pretty much my life."

RENEE COPE

Former Miss Winston and Wife of Driver Derrike Cope

Renee Cope didn't plan to marry a race driver.

"I'd been working through college for a modeling agency in Greensboro, Marilyn's, where they hire Miss Winstons," she says. "I didn't know what Winston Cup racing was all about. I assumed it was a hobby. I met Sandy Fix, who'd been Miss Winston, and found out it wasn't cheesy. It was a great opportunity to travel and *maybe* find a career with one of the corporations in the industry."

Cope became Miss Winston in 1991, a post she held for a season and a half, and found the sport "immediately contagious. The people at R.J. Reynolds broadened my horizons, Dennis Dawson especially.

"It was taboo for Miss Winston to date anyone in racing, and I'd heard horror stories about these drivers. Derrike's a super nice guy, and we used to talk on the phone a great deal. But I wasn't really interested. He *wore me down*, I guess. We dated for a while, got engaged, and married.

"Ron and Jackie Pegram, who I admire, of Motor Racing Outreach were in charge of our wedding. They're always there for people, and Jackie gets the wives together to talk about the stresses of the sport—not having sponsorship, teams closing doors, not having as much success on the track as you'd like, missing races—and how to provide moral support."

Cope says the chief worries of most drivers' wives are that their husbands will lose their jobs or suffer serious injuries.

"Losing the ride is definitely a concern," she says. "You have contracts with race teams. However, I've found those contracts aren't necessarily binding. You have to keep in the back of your mind, 'This may not last.'

"The wives worry more about injuries than the drivers do. The worst moment would have to be at Atlanta [in March of 1998], when Derrike hit the wall a ton. When I got to the infield care center, there were so many people in the reception area that I immediately realized how serious it was. His short-term memory was gone, and that terrified me. He'd been in bad wrecks,

Opposite: When Renee Cope became Miss Winston in 1991, she says found the sport "immediately contagious." During the year and a half she served as Miss Winston, winning drivers were greeted in victory lane by Cope's smile. She is sitting on the pit wall at Bristol.

but never had it affected him to that point. I panicked, and one of the medics grabbed me and said, 'It's OK. Calm down.'

Although Renee witnessed her husband's worst accident, which required an overnight hospital visit, she hasn't been on hand for the highlights.

"I did not watch the Daytona 500 [or Derrike's other 1990 victory at Dover]," she says. "I wasn't there when he won the pole [in 1998 at Charlotte] or the Busch race at New Hampshire. I haven't gotten to go to victory lane with him, but that's going to happen.

"It's difficult to live a *normal* life with the Winston Cup schedule—normal, to me, means being off and home on the weekend and working Monday through Friday," she adds. "We have friends *outside* the industry, so that's kind of our tie to a normal life. Everybody says, 'You have December and January off.' December might be broken up by appearances. January is probably the month when race teams are home the least because of testing. The sport has grown by leaps and bounds. I just hope they don't add more races. It's hard to go on vacation when you're married to a Winston Cup driver. People say, 'Every week's a vacation.' We get to travel, but he's working. It's not like we go sightseeing.

"He's usually got an appearance on race morning in the hospitality tents. A lot of times, we have a golf tournament for charity on Thursday, a sponsor obligation Friday night, another sponsor obligation Saturday night. You always see Morgan Shepherd, Brett Bodine, Derrike, at charity functions. Dale Jarrett does a great deal of the golf tournaments. You do not always see the big names. Perhaps they have obligations with sponsors. The charity functions are for a good cause, and Derrike's very dedicated to that. He's totally genuine, honest, upstanding, always wants to help others, always willing to go the extra mile. He likes to dress up and go to those more than I do. He has to push me a little. Once we're there, I'm glad he does. You meet a lot of interesting people, a lot of them new to racing. That's fun. It's neat to hear their questions about the industry and what Derrike does for a living. Derrike is very talented in getting

"A big misconception is how glamorous and wonderful it is. I'm not complaining, but it's like everything else in life—good and bad. During the summer, when you're home three days and gone four, it seems all you do when you're home is laundry."

in front of a crowd of corporate executives or fans. Everybody is mesmerized by him.

"There's not much free time when we travel. Most of our day is planned by obligations with sponsors, race team, or charity functions. There are towns where we've made friends who don't work in the industry. We'll try to go to dinner with them at the old standbys, Red Lobsters and Outbacks, or grill at the track. We socialize a little in the motorcoach area. On race day, I'll watch from the pits or motorhome, depending on the track.

"A big misconception is how glamorous and wonderful it is. I'm not complaining, but it's like everything else in life—good and bad. During the summer, when you're home three days and gone four, it seems all you do when you're home is laundry."

When Renee is home, her primary activity is caring for her three horses—the reason she hasn't been on hand for Derrike's most recent milestones. "Derrike and I are both very independent," she says. "I've had horses all my life, and he's had racing all his life. He's really understanding about allowing me to go to horse shows and not always be at the track."

Still, Renee says the "flexibility of being able to travel with him" is one of the better perks of Derrike's occupation.

"Not everybody is allowed to sit in the office with their husband at work," she says. "In a way, I am. You have an opportunity to be together a lot, but quality time together is different."

One reason is that fans recognize her husband "everywhere we go. On our honeymoon in Aruba, we came into the lobby, and people yelled, 'Derrike Cope!' They were from South Carolina—*big* race fans. Tourists would come up and ask, 'Are you Derrike Cope?' For the most part, the fans are really nice. A lot will say, 'I'd love to have your autograph, but I'll wait until after you eat.' But it's not a problem. We're glad to have them."

Above: Derrike and Renee Cope relax before the 1997 DeVilbiss 400 at Michigan in which Derrike finished 16th.

Renee is often recognized even when her husband isn't around.

"I've got [Miss Winston] trading cards. I do TV work, *Around the Track,* for Creative Sports Management," she says. "People say, 'We saw you on television!' I get embarrassed by the way they treat you. They kind of put you on this pedestal of, 'You're married to him!' He's the one who has the cool career. I'm just married to him. Don't get me wrong. It's wonderful. I love him to death. But don't be afraid of us. We're just normal, everyday people."

Jimmy Cox
NASCAR Official

"I love stock-car racing," says Jimmy Cox. "I waited too late in life to do what I *really* wanted to do, and that's be in racing.

"In 1976, a good friend I admire, [former NASCAR Busch Series Director] Ray Hill, told me NASCAR had discharged the stop-and-go man and asked if I wanted to go to Daytona and help. I was working for the Department of Corrections in North Carolina—a very depressing job. I turned in my resignation and never regretted it."

Cox's race-day duty in 1999 was supervising Winston Cup spotters, "making sure they understand what's going on," one of many tasks he has performed for NASCAR.

"We usually get to the track on Thursday, and I'd rather be an hour and a half early than 10 minutes late. We set up the equipment, unload the truck, get the scales set up, get everything ready. I measure pit road, make sure all the marks are there," he says. "I really enjoy parking the trucks on Friday morning. After we get the transporters parked, I check the roll bars and frame rails on the cars to make sure they're the right thickness. I've worked in the template room, pumped engines, [inspected] fuel cells, but the [primary] job I do is supervise pit road, take care of practice sessions, make sure the cars are lined up in order for qualifying, then send the cars off to qualify. Nothing makes me happier than to put that uniform on. It's a very enjoyable job."

That doesn't mean it's devoid of problems, however.

"One of my big gripes is rest-room facilities in the garage," Cox says. "It seems they have to add 10,000 seats to get another bathroom. Homestead has rest rooms everywhere. It is a *really nice* facility. The track that's not as accessible to spotters as it should be is Richmond. We have to go down two or three floors to the bathroom. We try to go during a caution.

"Travel is the worst part, although I've had time to see the Grand Canyon several times when we were in Phoenix. You're gone a lot. You have to have a very understanding family. It's a big thrill to talk to your grandchildren on Monday and Tuesday, and they say, 'I saw you on TV.' It makes the travel, eating fast food on the road, and driving all night worth it.

"When [former NASCAR Competition Director] Bill Gazaway had control, everybody respected him, but we didn't make a lot of money back then. Bill asked me one time, 'You got any

> **Opposite:** Jimmy Cox, leaning against the pit wagon of the Hendrick Motorsports team at New Hampshire, is usually among the first to know when something happens on pit road.

problems?' I said, 'I wondered if there's any chance of getting a few more bucks than we're mak-ing.' He put his arm around me and said, 'Jimmy, you see all the monkeys on that fence? Any of them would take your job for nothing.' They *think* they'd like it. But not many folks in the stands would give up their family life and live in a different motel every week."

Cox's spotter post, high above the grandstands, removes him from pit road and victory lane, two longtime haunts that produced both treasured and em-barrassing memories.

Opposite: Before a race at Pocono, Earl Barban and Cox review the NASCAR liability waiver forms that each team must sign at every race. Barban is the jackman and assistant engine tuner on Rusty Wallace's team.

"Until 1999, I used to go to victory lane. One of the happiest times of my life was being in the winner's circle with Ward Bur-ton when he won at Rockingham [in 1995]," Cox says. "He hugged everybody. That was *really* neat. Ward and Jeff are *close.* They remind me of me and my brother, Boyd, a living example of the type person I'd like to be—good dude, 230 pounds, 6-3, arms like tree limbs, redheaded, freckled-face like Huckle-berry Finn.

"Until 1999, I did the stop and go [signal], which was very exciting," he says. "At Daytona and Talladega, when they'd come down pit road running 150 miles an hour, they'd scare the shirttail right out of your britches. Pit-road speed is the best thing that ever happened. The most embarrassing thing was at Charlotte Motor Speedway. Rusty Wallace came down pit road under a caution. They forgot to put his hood pins in. I slowed him down, put all four pins in, and thought, 'What have I done?' I should have made him back up. They've got a picture of me with my paddle between my legs putting his hood pins in. Rusty *laughed.* There never were any repercussions. There could have been."

Cox plans to retire before the end of the 2000 season, but he isn't necessarily eager.

"From New Hampshire to Homestead to Sears Point, there are people I see once or twice a year I won't see anymore, and I'll miss them," he says. "I feel I've contributed a little something to NASCAR. I've never done anything to give NASCAR a black eye. I'm happy I got involved. I wish I had 20 more years."

"At Daytona and Talladega, when they'd come down pit road running 150 miles an hour, they'd scare the shirttail right out of your britches."

BILL ELLIOTT
Former Winston Cup Champion

Bill Elliott calls the highlight of his career "winning the championship in '88."

On 50 other occasions, a Winston Cup champion has been crowned. But no other driver has experienced a season like Elliott's 1985 campaign. That's when the Dawsonville, Ga., native authored more records than Sinatra, including 11 superspeedway victories and poles; captured the Winston Million in its inaugural season; became "Awesome Bill From Dawsonville," and put stock-car racing on the map.

"The sport was changing radically," he recalls. "It was starting to become a national sport, getting a lot more TV time. I didn't have any idea what came with it. I did some stuff the bull-headed way. I absolutely didn't know how to deal with a lot of stuff that was thrown at me, and there weren't a lot of people who could advise me because they'd never [dealt with] it. I had a *real* hard time.

"When I was in high school, I couldn't get in front of three people and say two words. I'm a very private, shy person. If I meet a stranger, I can't be open."

Yet "Million Dollar Bill" was bombarded by a growing legion of fans who'd been introduced to the sport via television and a host of media who didn't know a fan belt from a lug nut, but were drawn by his magical mystery tour of the nation's superspeedways.

Opposite: Bill Elliott celebrated his 25th year in NASCAR in 2000. During that period, fans voted him Winston Cup racing's Most Popular Driver a record 14 times.

"The race car was my sanctuary then. That's where I could escape," he says. "I still get nervous doing a lot of this stuff. It's something I've had to learn. I've grown into it."

The 14 times Elliott has been voted NASCAR's Most Popular Driver testify to how well he has learned to accept fame and fortune.

"I admire people who can handle different circumstances, be in control, and have a good attitude," he says. "I watched an A&E special on Danny Thomas. He became successful and was able not to lose focus, not lose sight of his family, and did a lot of good—like St. Jude's Hospital for children. I admire people who become successful, but don't lose sight of where they came from. I got into racing because I love to race. It wasn't for the money, the fame."

In fact, when he began his Winston Cup career, Elliott "didn't feel ready."

"When I started running at Dixie Speedway, my dad had vision. He led me to Winston Cup," Elliott says. "I didn't have the experience of some kids today. It's not uncommon for

kids to come into racing in their early twenties and have run literally hundreds of races. Jeff Gordon and Tony Stewart are perfect examples. When I started running eight or 10 NASCAR races a year in the late '70s, that's *all* I'd run. I'd only run short tracks a couple of years, so it was quite a learning curve.

"In 1980, Harry Melling gave us $500 to put his name on the car at Charlotte, and that was a big deal then. A Goodyear tire now is nearly $500. When we ran well at Charlotte and sat on the outside pole at Atlanta, Harry realized we might have potential. We asked if he'd sponsor our car. He paid us $25,000 for 12 races in 1981. That's when the cars downsized from a 115- to a 110-inch wheelbase—quite an expensive change, especially with no more money than we had.

"Melling was sponsoring Bud Moore's car. A lot of races, we finished better. They usually ran better, but had trouble or didn't finish. Harry decided he'd quit sponsoring Bud and buy what Daddy had—

Opposite: Although he hasn't won since 1994, Elliott, who signs autographs at Michigan, is still adored by his fans.

which was nothing. All I needed was a torch, a disk grinder, and a big hammer, and I could fix anything. We ran 22 races in '82 for Harry, all the races in '83. I wanted to succeed. That's what the whole family wanted. Harry never really put pressure on us, and it took Harry to be able to put it all together. [Brothers] Ernie, Dan, and I worked *extremely hard,* just like anybody else I've ever seen succeed in anything. I was totally dedicated. All I wanted to do was drive a race car, and I *understood* a car very well. I took more pride in that than driving. At the end of '83, we won our first race. In '84, I won three, and that set up the season I had in '85.

"After the '80s, we experienced some burnout within the family. I went to Junior Johnson, a productive three years I enjoyed," Elliott says of his six-victory tenure from 1992-94. "Junior was getting a little burned out on racing. I was with Budweiser, and I'd been with Coors for many years. I needed a change. I'd had an association with McDonald's for years, and it fell in place.

"Owning—slash—driving the car was the right thing to do in '95. I don't necessarily agree that's the way to go today. I don't dislike where I am, but that trend has changed. Sponsors now are looking more at multi-car entities. I don't know if that's good, because usually a multi-car team has only one car winning, and nobody else does squat."

One positive aspect of Elliott owning his team is job security.

"It's wild, but it's never gone through my mind my whole career that I might lose my ride," Elliott says. "The hardest part today is finding the right people, just like any major-league sport—football, baseball, whatever.

"I try to stay pretty active as far as the car's concerned. NASCAR has made a lot of safety advances, but the most significant change on the cars has been radial tires. They're faster because they keep the surface of the tire flatter on the pavement. It's a different feel.

"Technology's changing so fast now that you need a room full of engineers. People come in with different ideas that cost a lot. If you've got $100 million, you're going to spend it trying to get that extra hundredth or thousandth of a second faster. Say it costs $100,000 to build a race car. Let's say I can go to Atlanta and run 165 mph. Well, this guy comes in with a specialty part. It's going to cost $5,000 to buy. I might go from 165 to 170. To gain another horsepower might cost $100,000. To gain another might cost $500,000. You're looking for hundredths and thousandths of a second and need the insight to say, 'I'll spend $100,000 here or $50,000 there, or this is going to get us where we need to be.' That's where I feel I've lost a little control—a see-the-future-type deal. I don't understand where it's going."

Elliott's Hall of Fame resume includes 49 poles and 40 victories, including two in the Daytona 500, but he hasn't won since the 1994 Southern 500, his third triumph in NASCAR's oldest superspeedway race. And "the worst moment of my career—breaking my leg at Talladega [in 1996]" came after he became his own boss.

"It *really doesn't* bother me," he says of the drought. "I understand the roller coaster goes up and down. If I can run good, be in the hunt, and know I'm still competitive inside, I'll get there. I'm not going to worry about it. I have my ups and downs, but I still enjoy driving a race car. I also enjoy the people I've got working for me, and I've acquired a lot of good friends and fans."

Despite what he experienced in 1985, Elliott says the demands on his time now are "worse because the sport has grown."

"Sponsors back then put $1 million in the deal. Now it's $8 million, $10 million, whatever you can get," he says. "They're putting a lot of money into the business, and they expect more. You've got to do a lot of appearances, a lot of stuff to earn that money, whether you perform on the track or not."

Elliott not only thinks he is better equipped to deal with fame and fortune than he was 15 years ago, but to find time for a personal life.

"You put it in perspective and prioritize," he says. "Certain things are necessary. You've got to rest, eat right, spend as much time with your family as possible. The race tracks have gotten better, and NASCAR has gotten a lot more family friendly. I'm fortunate now that my family goes to 99 percent of the races.

"The biggest thing that's helped us in the past seven or eight years is we've been able to buy aircraft and fly our crew to races. It's important for those guys to get home at a decent time. I sympathize with that."

There's a notable change Elliott doesn't endorse: more people who are entering the sport in search of financial gain.

"I get disheartened when I see people coming into racing with the reasons they're coming in today versus 10 years ago," he says. "I don't like people who put material things first. Some people are getting too greedy, but I'm from a different era."

BENNY ERTEL
Business Manager for Mark Martin

"I have what Dale Earnhardt calls street smarts," says Benny Ertel, Mark Martin's business manager. "No class teaches you to become a business manager, to market Winston Cup racing. I'm not afraid to call anybody, including the president. What are they going to do? Hang up? Say no? I made my biggest deal on a cold call—Bobby Allison.

"I was sports critic for the ABC affiliate in Milwaukee—Benny the Bouncer—sold cars during the day, owned a pub, worked that at night. Jimmy Fennig, who is now Mark's crew chief, and I grew up in Milwaukee. Jimmy and his brother built me a race car. Jimmy said, 'We need somebody to drive the Slinger Nationals. Call Bobby Allison. He won the [1982] Daytona 500.' I called information in Hueytown, Alabama. Bobby didn't have an unlisted number. Bobby got on the phone. It freaked me out. I invited him for the Slinger Nationals and said [Wisconsin car owner] Gerry Gunderman might supply him with a car. He said he'd like that.

"I went to Hueytown, and Bobby told [longtime Allison employee] Donny Johnson, 'Order some headers, and see if we can get a better price.' I said, 'We can probably get them for free. We'd have to do an endorsement or something. Being Jewish, *there's no way I pay retail for anything.* Either I get it wholesale or free. So Bobby said, 'Let Benny call.'

"Bobby asked, 'Could you help me book appearances and short-track races?' Jimmy became crew chief for Bobby's short-track program, and I gave up driving to be Bobby's team coordinator. I met all the drivers through Bobby. Earnhardt went to Bobby and said, 'Do you think Benny can help me?' He said, 'That's up to Benny.' I said, 'I can do that.' "

With partners Tom Kincaid and Rich Rubenstein or by himself, Ertel recalls that he subsequently represented "Bobby, Dale, Rusty Wallace, Ken Schrader, Geoff Bodine, Harry Gant, Tim Richmond, Neil Bonnett, Davey Allison, Alan Kulwicki, Joe Nemechek, Dale Jarrett, Ernie Irvan, Kyle Petty, Sterling Marlin, Jimmy Spencer, Benny Parsons, Robert Yates, Richard Childress, Miller Brewing Company, GM Goodwrench, AC Delco, Kodak, Western Steer, Mac Tools, and, of course, Mark. Anything we did, they paid us 10 percent."

A decade before Martin hired Ertel as his business manager, Ertel was instrumental in hiring his current employer.

"Gerry wanted to go ASA racing," he recalls. "Jimmy said, 'We need a driver. I want

Mark.' I said, 'I called B.A. I can call Mark.' Mark took the gig and won the ASA champion-ship with Jimmy as crew chief in 1986.

"In '94, NASCAR was really taking off. Everybody was looking for somebody more personal. Mark decided to go with a full-time business manager."

Ertel was hesitant, however, when Martin mandated moving from North Carolina to Daytona Beach, Fla. "I said, 'If something goes sour, I'm stuck. If I need a job, racing's up here,'" Ertel recalls. "Mark said, 'You're with me as long as you want.' The only way I could lose my job is if I lied to Mark or stole from him. I don't plan on doing either.

"Representing Mark is easy. Bobby was a prince, and Mark's from the same mold. I go to 80 percent of the races—all the bigger tracks. A typical day at the track is meeting with anybody we're doing business with. I *love* making deals. *Ninety-nine percent of our deals are done at the track,* so you've got to be around.

"A typical day at home is meeting Mark at 7:30 [a.m.]—finding what Mark wants, then making that happen. Whatever he needs, I take care of. I've helped him purchase airplanes, land, homes, hangers. I'll run to Home Depot for him. I'll get his lunch. The man says, 'I need a lawn mower,' not a problem. *Whatever he asks for.* He can call me any time day or night, which he doesn't. He respects everybody else's time, because he wants people to respect his. He doesn't have much time to give. By June 15, we'll be booked for the season and looking at next year.

"My schedule book's my Bible. The schedule is the toughest part. But it's not tough for me. It's tough for Mark. I don't do a pimple of the stuff Mark has to do. It's *my* job to make it *easy* for him. I say, 'They wanted you in Michigan on Wednesday. I changed it to Thursday because you're there anyway. When you land at the airport, knock out the interview. He says, '*You the man.*' One thing I find difficult is when somebody tells me I'll have something tomorrow and it doesn't show up for two weeks. Tell me two weeks. Don't tell me something just to soothe me."

Ertel admits he's had "a lot of worst times" in racing and that two stand out, including Allison's career-ending wreck at Pocono in 1988.

"I spotted for Bobby," he says. "He said, 'I've got a right rear tire going flat.' It shredded. I said, 'Bobby, you OK?' Nothing. I knew there was a problem, that gut feeling you get. I got to the hospital and didn't see his beautiful gold watch. I go to the Stavola brothers and look inside the car. The watch is broken in the car. I got the watch fixed. Bobby was in the hospital a long time. They told me Bobby was released. I had a tumor on my kidney. I was in the hospital. I left, went to Hueytown, and took Bobby's watch. I said, 'What time is it?' He said, 'I don't know where my watch is.' I gave him the watch, and we visited for hours. I went back to the hospital, and a day and a half later, I was operated on.

"In 1991, I had a son on June 12. June 27, we're at Talladega. [Wife] Cheryl's in Daytona Beach

and calls Earnhardt during practice and told him my son, Max, lost his life. I'm with Rusty working on endorsements and bookings. Earnhardt comes flying in the trailer, kicks the door open. He said, 'Come with me now! I've got to put you on a plane.' Dale got his pilot, and we went to Daytona. Max got a virus and was too young to fight it. The day at Talladega was the worst."

The best?

"Rings from the eight championships I've been involved with and winning the Daytona 500 [with Allison in 1988] are memories you don't forget," he says. "When I married Cheryl in December of 1987 at the Speedway Club in Charlotte, Bobby and Jimmy shared best-man duties, and we had so many drivers and crew members we could have had a stock-car race."

Ertel's pit crew for his driving finale was equally star-studded.

Opposite: **His role as business manager for Mark Martin, Ertel says, is to make life easy for Martin. At New Hampshire in 1997, they review the weekend's schedule of events.**

"Bobby got Miller to sponsor a Baby Grand car for me at Charlotte in 1987 with him as crew chief," he recalls. "I said, 'I'll get my crew.' Davey and Kulwicki handled front tires, Wallace and Richmond rear tires, Kyle and Michael Waltrip the gas, Bobby Hillin's the jackman, Joe Ruttman's handing me Gatorade, Bonnett's working the sign board, Hank [Jones, president of Sports Design] the windshield, Earnhardt's scoring the car, and Parsons is my spotter. I qualify seventh. I spin. Richmond takes the tire off. Rusty picks up the tire and puts the same tire back on. Another time, Bobby says, 'Bring it in. Left-side tires.' I come flying in. The Gatorade pole comes in, and there's a roll of toilet paper on it. They kept messing with me. I caused five cautions and finished 12th. I said, 'I'm not driving anymore.' "

Ertel says it's difficult to balance family life with Winston Cup racing, but thinks he manages better than most.

"The guys working the souvenir trailer to the guys on pit crews work a tremendous amount of hours," he says. "Not many people work 70, 80 hours a week. I can't believe the labor laws haven't stepped in. I'm lucky, because Bobby and Dale always invited Cheryl [to races] because they had private aircraft. The same with Mark. When my 11-year-old daughter, Samantha Allison Ertel, who's named for Bobby, is out of school, they go to some races. At home, we play golf, ride bikes."

When his family isn't with him at races, Ertel usually is with Jones.

"We stock Hank's motorcoach with food. He'll sit back and watch old Benny boy cook. Hank is an unbelievable businessman—the *king* of souvenirs," Ertel says. "Hank had the vision to get ready for what was going to happen—bigger warehouse, more trailers, inventory, people. Hank took [Earnhardt's] souvenir program from zilch to a multimillion-dollar business.

"And this sport's just going to get bigger. What the owners, promoters, and France family have done with the facilities is awesome, because they've finally figured out how to get 200,000 people in the tracks."

MYRA FAULKENBURY
Credentials Manager, Lowe's Motor Speedway

Myra Faulkenbury estimates that 12,000 to 14,000 people attend each Winston Cup race at Lowe's Motor Speedway without purchasing a ticket. As Credentials Manager at the Concord, N.C., track, it's her responsibility to give those people the necessary access to perform their jobs—and to ensure no one is unnecessarily given that passage.

Faulkenbury's estimate of those granted credentials for a Winston Cup race "could be off, but I don't think it's low. That's workers, media—everybody with a credential that would get them through the gate."

But don't think you can simply talk your way inside.

"You hear all kinds of stories," she says. "Maybe I'd like to believe their story. There are a lot of people I might want to help but can't. I have guidelines, and the company has policies. Sometimes you can't help people because they *really* don't have a clue, and maybe they're in the wrong place or trying to pull a fast one. And I would rather err on the side of letting somebody in that pulled one over on me—and they're going to have to be pretty good to pull one over now—than risk alienating a *Sports Illustrated*, a *New York Times*. We don't send people away. I say, 'Give me a minute. Let me make some calls.' What I stress to my staff is be courteous, friendly, kind, patient, and professional.

"You've got to have safety factors in your credentials," she adds. "It's like my printer, Gary Smith, taught me, 'If I can print it, somebody else can.' But make it as hard as you can for somebody on the street. For example, I make sure I'm not duplicating the colors from the last race. I had a printer call me one time. Somebody had taken passes to him and asked if he could duplicate them. He wouldn't, which I admire."

Opposite: Myra Faulkenbury, Credentials Manager at Lowe's Motor Speedway, with an assortment of credentials.

Sorting through thousands of credential requests begins months in advance.

"People don't realize how long it takes to sell all these tickets two or three times a year, do credentials, and take care of the media—to put on the *quality* show we put on," she says. "That's the biggest misconception people have about the sport: 'So you put on the race? What do you do the rest of the year?' We have tons of paperwork we process and tons of letter writing we do.

"If a request is from people I know, like *Winston Cup Scene, Winston Cup Illustrated*, I refer to the last race. That helps me know what to give them. The newer ones and some of those that just don't look right, I'll meet with Jerry [Gappens, the speedway's Vice President of Promotion & Public Relations] and discuss them. One of the best things that's happened since I started is NASCAR giving the main media members annual credentials. That makes it easier for us and easier for them to do their jobs. When I started, there was just *Winston Cup Scene, Speedway Scene*, and *National Speed Sport News*. Now, we're getting more sponsors in the sport. We're working with more trade papers and magazines. The biggest unknown territory now is the Internet, trying to weed out people who want to be media outlets from people who really serve a purpose.

"The biggest problem I have is other people not doing their jobs so I can do mine. I have deadlines. Some people don't adhere to them.

"Race week is the toughest part because you've got all the people coming in [to the credential office]. The lines are 15 minutes, 20 tops. My first race, the lines were 45 or 50 minutes. I was scared to death. I was most afraid of people wanting credentials. But I found everybody wants a parking pass. They're more valuable than credentials. It blew my mind! Once I made it through that race, I had a feel for what I was facing.

"Our phones and fax don't stop race week. On night events, I usually open at 10 a.m., close the credential office at 7 or 8, and go to the press box. So it's 2 in the morning before I leave. The mornings I open at 10, I'm here at 8:30 because I don't want to get stuck in traffic. The days NASCAR is here at 7 a.m., I'm open at 7. It's a lot of 7 o'clock mornings and a lot of late nights. Sometimes you've worked so hard you don't want to eat. Race weeks are nice in that I usually lose a few pounds.

"You hear all kinds of stories. Maybe I'd like to believe their story. There are a lot of people I might want to help but can't. Sometimes you can't help people because they really don't have a clue."

"I couldn't devote the time I devote to this place if I didn't love it. I do think my children, who are 19 and 23, have suffered. As a single mother, I couldn't have done what I've done without my family."

"You work *so* hard to do well, get everything done, get all the people in who need to work that, when that checkered flag falls, it's a letdown.

"I couldn't devote the time I devote to this place if I didn't love it. I do think my children, who are 19 and 23, have suffered. As a single mother, I couldn't have done what I've done without my family. My first October race [in 1992], I didn't know what I was doing yet. It was 7 on a Saturday night in August, and my son called and said, 'Mom, are you *ever* coming home?' I packed up my stuff, took it home, and worked until midnight. But I was *home*.

"I want to know how you could have a social life on this job, but I *do* enjoy my job. I feel like I've found my niche. There's not another field I want to go into. I feel good about what I do. There's a lot of satisfaction in doing your job well, like helping Make-a-Wish Foundation children with terminal diseases. Seeing that kid that may not be here this time next year get an autograph from his favorite driver and knowing you helped make that happen, that's really satisfying.

"It's been a big confidence boost to be in this job," says Faulkenbury, who was assistant ticket manager before she assumed control of credentials. "I learned a lot from Phyllis Lipford [the speedway's Director of Ticket Sales]. She was a great role model and teacher, as much a friend as a boss. She was willing to give me up because it was in my best interests. I admire Humpy [Wheeler, the speedway's President and General Manager]. He's a visionary and promoter, and he really cares about people. The best moment I've had was in a staff meeting after my first race doing credentials. Humpy told me he'd heard lots of good things, but that he didn't want to say anything until after the race in case I was giving away the house. But that wasn't a problem because I came from the ticket office, where we were *selling, not giving* them away."

ELI GOLD
TV and Radio Broadcaster

If Eli Gold's voice is the most recognizable in motorsports, it's the realization of a longtime ambition.

"My eighth-grade yearbook said: Future Occupation—sports broadcasting. I knew what I wanted," Gold says. "I used to be an office boy at Madison Square Garden. My pay was a press pass to every event at the Garden—Ali-Frazier, seventh game of the NBA Finals. I was there with my tape recorder, practicing play-by-play. I delivered mail to Bob Wolff, the broadcaster for the Knicks. He would listen to the tape I'd made the previous night—Rangers, Knicks, college ball—and say, 'You're doing this well. You're doing that poorly. Work on this.' I'd take notes and try to do better.

"Growing up in Brooklyn, on *Wide World of Sports*, you'd see 10 laps from Darlington between wrestling and cliff diving. I was attracted by what I saw. In 1975, I was broadcasting hockey with the Long Island Ducks, the lowest rung. Have you seen the movie *Slapshot*? That was the league. Traveling on the Ducks' bus, I heard NASCAR on the radio and thought, 'I'd love to do that.' I found out there was this thing called Motor Racing Network. I wrote and said I'd like to work for them. I followed up with a phone call. Jack Arute, then the general manager, said, 'Have you done any racing announcing?' I said, 'Certainly.' I'd never been to a NASCAR race in my life. He said, 'Send me a tape.' I waited three days, called back, and said, 'I can't find my [non-existent] racing tapes. Would you take a hockey tape?'

"I was within two-and-a-half years of making it in the National Hockey League as an announcer for the St. Louis Blues. I guess he figured if I could keep up with the speed of hockey, I might be able to keep up with racing. He called back and said, 'I'll bring you to Charlotte for the World 600. If you do well, we'll keep you. If you stink, you can go home.' I was on the air in May of '76 for an on-the-air audition, which today you'd never do. I worked turns one and two. I remember whoever led the first lap would get the unheard-of sum of $1,000. I remember my call, 'And they're running for the *big money*—$1,000 to lead the first lap.' I never imagined then

Opposite: **From atop the main tower, Eli Gold welcomes his audience on The Nashville Network to a 1999 telecast from Phoenix. Rookie Tony Stewart won the race, the second of his three 1999 victories.**

in my wildest dreams NASCAR would be where it is today. I'm not a visionary. I admire the France family. Thankfully, they were visionaries."

Gold subsequently teamed with Barney Hall as MRN's anchor tandem. "If I had a mentor, it would be Barney, taking me under his wing, introducing me to people," says Gold, who still juggles MRN assignments with his duties as play-by-play announcer for The Nashville Network's NASCAR and drag-racing telecasts and as the voice of the Alabama Crimson Tide in football and basketball.

"I came to Birmingham in 1977 to broadcast the World Hockey Association," he says. "Then the Double-A baseball team came to town, and I did its games for four years. Thirteen years ago, the Alabama job opened. The university and my NASCAR employers have worked well together. I cannot miss an Alabama football game. Alabama knows the importance of SpeedWeeks. TNN respects the importance of the NCAA Tournament and SEC Tournament.

"I have not found a way to compare sitting at the start/finish line broadcasting the Daytona 500 to sitting at the 50-yard line at the Sugar Bowl for the national championship. They're both huge, but so different. I'm more tied up in my gut to Alabama. You're broadcasting for their fans. You care who wins. One of the best nights was the Alabama national championship game [a 34-13 conquest of Miami for the 1992 title]. The electricity in the Superdome was almost beyond description. When you're doing a NASCAR race, you're broadcasting for fans of 43 drivers. You want to see a good, safe race and don't really care who wins.

"I stayed in the [MRN] anchor seat until 1996, when the opportunity was presented to move to television, which I swore I'd never do. I was going to be a lifer on radio. In television, you're putting captions on pictures—not as easy as it sounds. But you don't have to describe the pewter gray sky, whereas on radio you do. That's a wonderful challenge. I appreciate the Walter Cronkites of the world, the pioneers of broadcasting. I've admired Marv Albert, who

"We get five faxes a week with every bit of information—useful or useless. At the same time, drivers are a little less accessible. It used to be you could walk in the garage, and there stood Richard Petty, Bobby Allison, David Pearson, or whomever."

obviously has had problems, and Bob Costas, a good friend for years. I admire his encyclopedic memory. I wish I was half the wordsmith he is.

"TV's where it's at. NASCAR's best change has been the advent of live television. That brought the sport into the living room of that guy in Pocatello, Idaho, who never used to go."

Finding time in Gold's hectic schedule for his wife, Claudette, and their daughter, Elise, "hasn't always been easy."

"On the air from New Hampshire, I said, 'Sweetheart, happy 22nd anniversary.' Buddy Baker [TNN's motorsports analyst] chimed in, 'That's why you've been married so long. You never see each other.' We see each other more than we used to," Gold says. "During the summer, the family travels with me a good bit, and they try not to miss a football game. At home, what free time I have, I do something with the family. The other night, we were watching Claudette plant roses. Whatever you do, do it as a family."

In 1997, Gold eliminated "getting up at 4:30 in the morning to catch a 6 a.m. flight 50 nights a year" from his travel schedule by broadcasting *NASCAR Live* every Tuesday night on "437 stations in 42 states" from a studio in his basement instead of Daytona Beach, Fla. "When I say, 'Goodnight everybody,' it's 6:58 Birmingham time. I wander upstairs 25 seconds later," Gold says.

"On the road, I'll grab dinner or go to a ball game," he adds. "I'm a sports fan. If we're in Michigan and the Tigers are home, you'll find me in Tiger Stadium on Friday night. If we're in New Hampshire, I'll go to Fenway. Major-league baseball would be a wonderful job. I've gone to preseason football games in the Pontiac Silverdome. I'd love to do the NFL just to say I've done it."

Gold's job isn't as easy as he makes it appear.

"We used to have to scramble for information about certain guys. The importance of sponsors getting their message out has heightened the accessibility of information. Now we get five faxes a week with every bit of information— useful or useless," he says. "At the same time, drivers are a little less accessible. It used to be you could walk in the garage, and there stood Richard Petty, Bobby Allison, David Pearson, or whomever. Many times now, the drivers are in their motorcoaches, staying out of the hustle and bustle.

Above: Gold, in the garage area at Pocono, says his job is "a magnificent way to make a living." Gold's first racing broadcast was an on-the-air tryout in the 1976 World 600 at Charlotte.

"What makes the job difficult is making sure you have all the information. I'm a news nut, not to the exclusion of watching reruns *of I Love Lucy* or *The Andy Griffith* Show, but when I'm home, it's CNN, headline news. I read voraciously—three or four newspapers a day, non-fiction, and biographies. I'll study my rear end off, because I'm not going to go on the

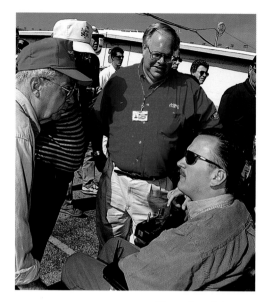

air and embarrass myself. You do all this homework and might use seven percent of it. But I'm not going to get lazy and give my employer a reason to fire me. No broadcast is difficult if you've done your homework."

It usually isn't, anyway.

"When there's a serious injury or fatality, I'll get sick to my stomach," he says. "And if my stomach gets sick, it affects two-thirds of my body. That's a big stomach. I feel nauseous, because you know these guys, their wives, their kids. I've had embarrassing moments. Once at Pocono, I said, 'Fellows, don't come to me for a while. I've got to take a leak.' All of America knew that, because I was on the air.

"I'm blessed with being able to go to the biggest sporting events in the world," Gold adds. "I get to broadcast, which I love. I'm on the air, but I'm not having to cover the war in Kosovo, the tragedy of Columbine High. But I'm still on in a serious vein. Alabama football is serious, and NASCAR is serious business to racing fans.

"You travel on someone else's ticket. The facilities have been upgraded immensely. Some of the old announcing booths were no bigger than a closet. Now, you're in first-class broadcast facilities. As you leave from calling the Daytona 500, the national championship football game, the U.S. Nationals in drag racing, or the NCAA round of 16, you go to your first-class hotel, the guy hands you a check and says, 'Thanks. See you tomorrow.' The whole thing is a magnificent way to make a living—like living in the candy store of life.

Above: Learning what's going on in the garage is important preparation for Gold's telecasts. He talks with former Top Fuel drag racer Darrell Gwynn at Daytona.

"When that opening music rolls, that adrenaline pumps. When it stops pumping, it's time to leave. Right now, it's still pumping gallons. I hope this continues forever."

"As you leave from calling the Daytona 500, you go to your first-class hotel, the guy hands you a check and says, 'Thanks. See you tomorrow.' The whole thing is a magnificent way to make a living—like living in the candy store of life."

FRANCES GOSS
Ticket Manager, Atlanta Motor Speedway

Frances Goss is rarely mentioned in the same sentence as Bill France Sr. or Daniel Boone, but perhaps she should be. Because Goss, Atlanta Motor Speedway's Ticket Manager since 1966, is a bona fide pioneer.

"I blazed a few trails, because when I came to the speedway, women who worked at a race track were not respected," Goss says. "There was a time we needed money counters. I went to the local banker and asked if I could use some tellers. He told me he would not *allow* his girls to work at a race track. I asked him, 'Am I any different than the girls who work for you?'

"When I first came, it was considered a redneck sport. It was just the Weaver Grandstand and the backstretch wooden bleachers. Fans would bring blankets and sit on the dirt bank. Women were not allowed in the pits except when the beauty queen went to victory lane. In the early days, you didn't worry about what was served in the concession stands or how many bathrooms you had. You did the bare minimum, and that was all. As women started getting into racing, the facilities started growing. The biggest change I've seen is, as sponsors came on the scene, racing started becoming more of a family sport—instead of just the guys.

"Bruton [Smith, Chairman of the Board of Speedway Motorsports Incorporated] told me even before he bought the track, 'Atlanta is a diamond in the rough. I'd like to see what could be done with this place.' The jobs that have been created, the upgrade of the facility—I would have never believed Atlanta Motor Speedway would look like it does today. Bruton has come a long way since 1990. We had seven full-time employees when the track was sold."

Goss's staff now includes eight full-time and a couple of temporary employees who work for six weeks prior to an event. Some 160 people are under her direction during race week, including ticket sellers, those who stub tickets, and security personnel at the track's 18 gates.

"We start getting ready for a specific event about six weeks out as far as preparation for crowds and gate sales," she says. "Scheduling personnel, finding enough personnel to do the job, is the toughest part.

"I come to work before anybody else to make sure the equipment is working. It takes 30 minutes to make sure the phones and computers are OK. It takes 20 minutes to reboot the computer system, and that 20 minutes is terrifying on race weekend. All it takes is one power glitch—somebody hitting a phone pole—and you're in trouble. You're putting out fires all the time. You never know what the public is going to present to you. I think because of the pricing of tickets, fans think we're rolling in money. But purses are so much higher now. The public demands nicer facilities. Demands for customer service are up. For years, we had a platform that would hold only five or six wheelchairs. We can accommodate 300 now. I think that speaks well for the facility and for fans who feel they can come out regardless of their physical status. That's what we push for: We want anybody to be able to come out.

"My average day is about 10 hours," adds Goss, who is married and has three grown children. "I'm from the old school. If I tell you I'm going to do a job, I'm going to see it through. If it takes all day, I don't go home until it's done. Sometimes it gets to be 16, 18 hours a day. It's usually just that six-week period prior to the race that's so demanding, and you try to schedule family life around that.

"A lot of people think it's exciting to work here because they're race fans. But the first thing you tell them is that they don't get to see the race, that if you're that addicted to racing, don't apply for this job. They really don't understand until they've worked through one race. Most people think if you work at a race track, you have free access to tickets. That's not the case. That's our bread and butter.

"You have to explain to employees that, at race time, we don't get ill and don't get short tempered. We just get short of words. We're just too busy for conversation. Seating problems show up within 30 minutes before or after the green flag falls. A lot of people don't get here until 1 o'clock, and if somebody happens to be in their seat, you have problems. People watching the race call to order tickets for some future race. The worst thing we generally have to do is deal with people who arrive after credentials close who show up at the ticket office thinking we can help them.

"You get so busy you forget to eat. You start eating a hamburger at 12 o'clock and finish it at 5. Stone cold. When you get lunch and somebody says, 'I need you,' you stop and put that fire out, whether it's a computer that won't work or an irate customer at the counter. But I enjoy people. More than anything else, that makes me enjoy working with the public.

Opposite: Although her average work day is about 10 hours, Frances Goss can be found in her office for as many as 18 hours a day as race week at Atlanta Motor Speedway approaches. The tickets she holds are for the season-ending NAPA 500.

"I've had a lot of help along the way," Goss adds. "I had a minister, Allen Phillips, who helped me get two years of college I would not have had otherwise. I have no idea what he saw in me, but I'm thankful he did. The person I admire and respect the most at this point is [Atlanta Motor Speedway President and General Manager] Ed Clark. He treats fans the way he'd like to be treated, and that makes my job 100 percent easier. Larry Hogan, the general manager when I first came to work during the years coming out of bankruptcy, took me under his wing. People who take care of fans are my kind of people, and he was one of those. If I ever had a mentor, it would have been [former co-owner] Walt Nix, because he actually expected me to take care of everything. And, if I couldn't, he'd say, 'Yes, you can.' And if I made a mistake, it was no big deal. I learned that mistakes aren't mistakes until you can't fix them. That's why I tell the girls here, 'You can't do anything that hasn't been done before, so don't worry. Do your job, and if you make a mistake, we'll fix it.' It makes for a more relaxed working atmosphere.

"I've had people tell me I've been their role model. I don't think of myself as that. I've done what I needed to do to survive. I enjoy problem solving. I feel the experience I have and being flexible—able to think on my feet—are assets. I feel as good as I did when I was 16."

MAX HELTON

Founder and Senior Chaplain, Motor Racing Outreach

When Max Helton moved from California to North Carolina in 1988 to start Motor Racing Outreach, he says that some people "thought I'd flipped my lid."

"I'd been a Baptist minister for 26 years, had churches in California, Chicago, and New York. There's security in pastoring a church—retirement money, nice house, good support system," says Helton, MRO's Founder and Senior Chaplain. "Norm Evans, a three-time All-Pro with the Miami Dolphins, started chapel services for the NFL. After he retired, he got into ministry and encouraged me that racing needed it, too. My family was used to unusual things in my ministry, like working with street gangs, so they had some idea that this dad and husband of theirs was a little wacky. But my church members thought I was crazy—stepping into a situation in which you have no financial guarantee.

"I went to a Winston Cup race at Riverside in 1987 with Winston West driver Rick McCray and met Darrell Waltrip. We became friends, and he encouraged me to do this. Darrell and Lake Speed have been a great inspiration. Their commitment to this ministry has meant a lot, and the No. 1 person I admire is my dad, a pastor who retired recently at age 83. But Norm's been a real mentor from the beginning of this ministry, and he's still the person I call."

Helton's ministry is a 'round-the-clock venture.

"The biggest misconception is that all we do is a chapel service on Sunday for 20 minutes," he says. "People don't realize the involvement we have in the lives of these people. We bring the church to them. Ron Pegram on our staff is a great coordinator. We have three 18-wheelers—a community center, a place for children to play, a fitness center. Outside the track, we have an 18-wheeler for fans, Racing Fans Outreach. We have a concert Saturday night, a service Sunday morning. Sometimes, a driver shares his testimony. Kyle Petty loves doing that. Kenny Wallace does it often. Bobby Hillin, Robert Pressley, Jeff Gordon, Michael Waltrip, Mike Dillon, Hut Stricklin, Darrell, and Lake have.

"Every Monday, I fly to Daytona Beach, where I have Bible study with Mark Martin and his wife, Arlene. Tuesdays, I teach four Bible studies—at 8 with Michael Waltrip, his dad, and Ron Stevens, who's been involved in racing; at 9:30 with Ernie and Kim Irvan; at noon

> **Opposite:** Moments before the start of the 1998 UAW-GM Quality 500 at Charlotte, Max Helton lends encouragement to Mark Martin, who went on to win the race. Martin is one of Helton's regular students in Bible study.

at Robert Yates Racing for the whole shop; Tuesday night for the racing community. On Wednesday, I come to the office and counsel—from marital counseling to dealing with being fired to emotional stress. I take Thursdays off, but sometimes I have to fly to a race. I hang out in the garage all day during race weekends. I can hardly be in the garage without somebody saying, 'I need to talk to you.' When we first started, hardly anybody would talk to me."

Since that has changed dramatically, Helton says it's "really hard to balance" family life and leisure with the demands of his job.

"In the midst of busy activity, to take a day, go somewhere, kick back, and do nothing, that's really wonderful, and I take my wife with me as often as I can, probably half [the races]," he says. "But what's normal? In the '20s and '30s, you worked 12 hours a day six days a week. In all human history, we never had 9-to-5 jobs until after World War II, and that's fallen by the wayside. Sometimes you even get too busy to eat. I've actually gone three days without eating."

At least his former congregation no longer thinks he's "crazy."

"When I go to West Coast races, some of those members come to our service," he says. "They're absolutely in shock at the congregation we have in Winston Cup racing, to see drivers involved, leading the service, leading a prayer. It blows their mind. So now they're very supportive.

"Racing's greatest change over the past 10 years has been the phenomenal growth, not only as far as fan base, but in the dollars it takes to operate," adds Helton, who has seen donations to his ministry increase dramatically. "Our budget in 1989 was $68,000. That's travel, salary—everything. In the last four years, our budget has grown from $370,000 to $3 million.

"As far as MRO is concerned, the biggest change is the community spirit. Ten years ago,

nobody had a motorcoach. Now, we're living side by side. It changes the dynamics of how you get along. It's made my job much easier. They're living next door to guys they're racing. Their kids play together. Their wives talk. I go to work with 100 percent of my congregation and 100 percent of my prospects three days a week, and I'm there at night. You're hanging out where they are. They'll say, 'Hey, Max, come chat.' We call it the 'Ministry of Hanging Out.' "

MRO is involved in 23 racing series and "has always been interested in racing anywhere in the world. What's incredible is the invitations we're getting from sanctioning bodies who want our services. We're working on establishing stuff in Europe, Australia, Southeast Asia. Our plan for the next five years is to cover the globe."

There is one aspect of his job that Helton dreads.

"*The* hardest thing is having to inform a wife that her husband has died. It doesn't get any harder than that," he says. "Probably *the* absolute toughest moment of my life was having to tell a wife who was parked on the side of the road on a cell phone that her husband died. It's hard enough face to face, holding her hand, and being a comfort. But on a phone? I said, 'There's no way this should happen in this setting.' "

Helton also finds it difficult to "say no to really good things, a real need, because time-wise, I can't do it. It tears at your heart."

But he's understandably proud of what MRO has accomplished.

"We're filling a need in the racing community," he says. "It's what He wants me to do. It's amazing the number of things that come your way from people who are hurting. At some point, you realize there's more to life than fame, popularity, or money. There's a vacuum we all have, and that vacuum can only be filled with God.

Opposite: Helton is particularly proud of Jeff Gordon's off-the-track accomplishments. Gordon was invited to share his testimony at a Billy Graham crusade.

"For 2,300 years, there has been a national champion somewhere in vehicle racing, starting with chariots. So I ask drivers, 'Who won the national championship in 1392?' Nobody knows. We don't even know 1892. Who's going to remember what you do 1,000 years from now? Nobody. What's going to count is eternity and the influence you have on others. It's tremendous to know you're helping stabilize a person's life, helping a person keep his sanity in the midst of pressure to perform.

"The highs you get are sitting in Bible study and having a driver tell you how much he's learning and how much more he wants to learn. I get pumped up to see a person's faith grow and realize how far he has come. I wish every fan could see what I see when I sit down with these guys. At Atlanta in 1997, three guys could have won the championship—Mark Martin, Dale Jarrett, or Jeff Gordon. After Bible study that Saturday night, we were in Mark's motorcoach. These three guys and I held hands, and they prayed out loud for each other to have a good day. That was an incredible experience. I don't think you'd have seen that a few years ago in this sport.

"I've heard Jeff say many times, 'Even though I love racing, racing has no higher thrill to me than my relationship with God. That is more important than what I do in that race car.' Jeff was invited to share his testimony at a Billy Graham crusade—a high moment in *my* life. Jeff struggled with it because he felt almost unworthy—a guy who, by his admission, before he came around MRO had no background with God. To know you've been a part of helping this individual is very satisfying. That makes it worthwhile."

JANE HOGAN
Caterer

"My husband [Larry] was an original investor in North Carolina Motor Speedway. One time we got rained out, and I ended up at my house cooking for 33 people, including James Garner and Dickie Smothers," Jane Hogan recalls. "Not long after that, Larry was looking for a caterer, and [former Tosco executive] Dick Dolan said, 'Call your wife.'

"After Larry and I divorced, I looked at my options. After 23 years as a housewife, your marketable skills are few. I figured catering was what I did best," says Hogan, who in the early '70s launched a catering business in Ellerbe, N.C., that specializes in Winston Cup racing. "A lot of people expected me to fail, and I knew I was not going to fail. This may sound immature, less than honorable, and all the adjectives you can think of, but when Larry got fired [as General Manager] at Atlanta [International Raceway] and I kept working, it was a pretty big moment. He insisted I'd never make it.

"For several years, I just did [Tosco's] suite. Then I had R.J. Reynolds, and I did the speedway's suite at Charlotte. Dick, [Speedway Motorsports Incorporated Chairman of the Board] Bruton Smith, and [Lowe's Motor Speedway President and General Manager] Humpy Wheeler gave me the opportunity.

"Humpy is one of the people I have a great deal of respect for. When Larry and I were getting divorced, [Wheeler] wrote me a very nice letter. I was impressed he cared enough to write. He's an extremely kind, caring man. I have a great deal of respect for [Tosco executive] Bill Joyner for a lot of the same reasons. I love Richard Petty. I like real gentlemen who care about people.

"It has been 25 years, and I still have the same customers I started with, and I've added others. I've always cooked for my customers like I cooked for my family. I will not serve anything I wouldn't want. You get meat, salads, vegetables, fruit. I want healthy meals. I don't want much starch and fat. I've worked with [clients] for so long that I know everybody's favorites. You entertain the people, get to know them, make them feel at home. They become like family.

"Every time I tell Bill I'm thinking about quitting, he shudders. I tell him that one of these days I'm going to drop dead in one of his VIP suites, and he's going to have to ship my body

Opposite: Jane Hogan, shown here in the Tosco corporate suite at Dover, began her business in the early '70s and still has most of her original customers.

home. [Atlanta Motor Speedway Ticket Manager] Frances Goss and I are probably the only women left who were around when I started. That means we're tough old broads.

"No normal human being would work the way I work at my age [66]," she adds. "Race week is always at least 20-hour days. That's because I have standards. You can buy anything in a can, carton, or plastic tubs. I don't. I make my own. That makes for long days. Last week, I got up Friday morning after having slept one-and-a-half hours. I went back to bed Monday morning at 3:30. I worked from 8 yesterday morning until 3 this morning, went to bed for two hours, got up, took a shower, put everything in the oven. Friends of mine where I go to church can't believe I work this hard. They ask why, and I say, 'That's what it takes to do the job the way I want to do the job.' I do this because I love it. It's not money that keeps me going. In preparation for a race, say Atlanta, I know there's a good chance the weather is going to be bad. I plan my menus so some food will keep. I'd rather take the loss [for purchasing too much food] than come up short."

Many of Hogan's specialties, including banana pudding, seafood salad, and egg salad, have become almost as legendary in Winston Cup garages, suites, and media facilities as Petty and Dale Earnhardt. So what does she eat at the track?

"I ate some meatballs and a spoonful of rice yesterday afternoon," she says. "When you cook that much, smell it, and see it, it just doesn't appeal to you."

Hogan says her job is easier than when she first started her business.

"I look back at the conditions under which I had to work and can't believe I got my job done, working out of the back of a truck because there was nowhere else," she says. "There weren't a lot of amenities. The worst time would probably be Atlanta when it snowed [in March of 1993], and all the water froze. We had to melt ice in the microwave to make coffee. My equipment has never failed me, but when the water and power go, it's like horse-and-buggy days.

Above: When Rusty Wallace captured his 50th Winston Cup victory at Bristol in the spring of 2000, he had "Mother No. 2" pose with him in victory lane.

"At established tracks, I never have a problem. You go to a new track, and the people who do not understand your job—like security people—make it hard sometimes. That's the only time I really get aggravated. I smile a lot, and it works out.

"One reason I've been here this long is because racing has become my family, and it's the mother in me that makes me want to take care of my family. I hate the bad wrecks that come with restrictor-plate racing. Those are my friends out there, my 'children,' so it really frightens me.

"Rusty Wallace calls his mother 'Mother No. 1' and me 'Mother No. 2.' I think the drivers are on the road so much they really like that, and I'm old enough that I'm not a threat to their families. Earnhardt announced one day to the press corps that I was going to make him an apple pie every time he won a race. This was news to me. Once I went to Europe and was gone for six weeks. When I got back, Earnhardt told me I owed him seven pies. He keeps track. Rusty found out I was making Earnhardt an apple pie, and he was jealous, so he wanted an apple pie. Bill Elliott likes cherry pies, so I've always made cherry for him—and banana pudding, because that's all he eats on race day. Jeff Gordon eats chocolate chip cookies. It's amazing. They've got all the money in the world, but they go silly over pies and cookies. If Earnhardt sees me coming, he'll stand on the back of the truck and start waving.

"There's an interesting story on why I call him Earnhardt. When they had the Dale-and-Dale show [Jarrett's narrow victory in the 1993 Daytona 500], I saw Earnhardt the next race and said, 'Dale, I prayed so hard.' I said, 'Lord, Dale has done so well at Daytona—won everything but the Daytona 500. Lord, he's really a good man. If you could let him win, it'd make him very happy.' But he told me, 'You forgot to tell the Lord which Dale. From now on, call me Earnhardt.'"

NED JARRETT

TV Broadcaster, Former Winston Cup Champion

Ned Jarrett calls broadcasting "a bigger challenge than driving a race car."

"Growing up on a farm, working at a sawmill, I never thought I'd get involved in broad-casting," says Jarrett, a two-time Winston Cup champion who has become one of the most successful commentators in motorsports. "I learned to drive very young, probably eight. When they started building Hickory (N.C.) Speedway, farmers and sawmillers would say, 'Wait un-til they get that thing built. I'll show them how to drive.' I thought, 'I ought to try that.' I drove in the first race at Hickory in '53. I finished 10th, which wasn't bad, having never been on a race track. I was so tired they had to help me out of the car. That was a 50-lap race, probably 18 miles. I couldn't believe I was so tired, because at the farm and sawmill I did a lot of physical labor. It was the mental part that tired me. Once I learned to relax in a race car, it was no problem driving whatever length the race might be."

Jarrett captured 50 Winston Cup victories, including 15 in 1964 and 13 a year later in a factory-supported Ford, before astonishingly announcing his retirement in 1966 at age 34.

"I lucked up and won the championship in '61, my second full year in the series," he says. "I didn't know how to represent myself, my family, my sport. My dad tried to instill in us to do your best at whatever you're doing, so I took the Dale Carnegie course. Once you've gone through the course, you *want* to talk. Writers and what few elec-tronic media were there started seeking me out for interviews. Plus, I won one race in '61, and that's *not* the way I wanted to do it. So I vowed I'd win the championship again.

"I wanted to spend more time with my family, and I'd accom-plished the goals I set. One was to win the Southern 500 at Darlington, because if you beat *that* track, it's a great feeling of accomplishment. I managed that in '65 by 14 laps and also won the championship.

> **Opposite:** The courteous and affable Ned Jarrett was nicknamed "Gentleman Ned" during his racing career. He has fashioned a second successful career in broadcasting since then and appears on three different networks.

"I was leading the points in April of '66 and was well on my way, I thought, to another championship. Richard Petty, a real role model and major asset to our sport, and I were at Darlington testing tires. They called me to a pay phone and said Ford Motor Company wanted to talk me. Ford had a double overhead cam engine it wanted to race, and NASCAR didn't approve it. So

"The best moment in my career period was the Daytona 500 in 1993 when Dale won," says Jarrett, who made a memorable call on CBS of his son's last-lap duel with Dale Earnhardt. "That supersedes anything I ever did."

Ford said, 'We'll take our toys and go home.' That got me thinking, 'How much security do you have in this business?' And I had vowed that however far up the ladder I got, I'd quit while I was there. I'm the only driver who ever retired while he was the reigning champion.

"When I announced my retirement, Bob Montgomery and Hank Schoolfield gave me the opportunity on the Universal Racing Network in the latter part of '66. Hal Hamrick, who became the anchor when Bob died, helped me make the transition to radio."

While making the transition from cockpit to broadcast booth, Jarrett also managed Hickory Speedway and Charlotte's Metrolina Speedway and did promotional work for Anheuser-Busch.

"I continued to broadcast all along and switched over to MRN," he says. "We started *[Ned Jarrett's] World of Racing* in 1978 with 12 stations. That was a losing proposition to begin with. I struggled to feed and educate the family, but we did. It was very tough from a financial standpoint, but at least I was spending time with my family.

"When Daytona was televised live by CBS in 1979, I was asked to serve on that team. Ken Squier opened that door for me. ESPN came into it in the mid-'80s. In fact, 1983 was the first year I was able to start saving for the future. It took that long to make a living from broadcasting."

Today, Jarrett is "the only person in the world who's on three networks," as a motorsports commentator on CBS and ESPN and with *Inside NASCAR* on The Nashville Network, and his radio show now has "about 325 stations."

Jarrett says his 17-year ordeal to make broadcasting profitable "wouldn't be as tough today. Winston started professionally promoting our sport, and television has been a major boost. The technology that allows various camera positions on the cars allows the fan to come closer to the sport. That helps make my job easier, because most of the time we've got a camera that can show what we're talking about. The facilities have improved, and that's helped make my job easier. Computer scoring has been a godsend. I don't know *how* we did broadcasts before.

"The toughest thing is the travel and getting where I need to go around the race track. People say, 'I'd love to have your job.' They envy me because I *get* to go to all the races. But now it's not 'get to.' I have to. It's not as much fun as it used to be. We're there when the track opens. We try to learn as much as we possibly can so we can talk reasonably intelligently when the time comes. Television has made me more recognizable. I'm flattered people want to stop and talk or get my autograph or have a picture made, but I've got a job to do. Traveling commercial airlines has become a big chore for the same reasons. You hate to be rude and say you don't have time, but if I had to travel commercial to every race, I'd quit."

Since Jarrett retired at 34 to spend more time with his family, it's logical to assume he has given his son, Dale, the 1999 Winston Cup champion, advice on balancing family and career. Ironically, it has been the other way around.

"It might even be tougher today to balance family with driving race cars," Ned says. "Dale works *hard* just trying to get an extra hour or two with his family. When he first talked about getting an airplane, I said, 'That doesn't make economical sense.' He kept saying, 'I can get a couple of extra hours with my family. I can be home and see the kids Sunday night.' Now, he allows me to fly with him, so I think he did *exactly* the right thing. Then he wanted a motorcoach. I said, 'That doesn't make sense. You can stay at the nicest hotels in the world.' Then, I could see he could bring the family and be with them at the track. Last year was the first year I used a motorcoach, and it'll probably extend my career. It's almost like home.

"The favorite times for [wife] Martha and I are when the whole family comes to our house Christmas, Thanksgiving, and Mother's Day. We don't talk much racing, even though Jimmy Makar [Bobby Labonte's crew chief] is married to [daughter] Patti. I also enjoy playing golf with [sons] Dale and Glenn [a TNN announcer and former driver] and being around the grandkids."

Jarrett's devotion to family is emphasized by the biggest thrill of his career.

"The best moment in my career *period* was the Daytona 500 in 1993 when Dale won," says Jarrett, who made a memorable call on CBS of his son's last-lap duel with Dale Earnhardt. "That supersedes anything I ever did."

BUCKSHOT JONES
Winston Cup Rookie

"Your rookie year is tough in any sport. It's like going back to school," says Buckshot Jones, who was enrolled in the school of hard knocks as a Winston Cup rookie in 1999.

"In Busch, you're running good every weekend. Go to Cup, and you're going to the back," he says. "The Cup races are longer, a lot tougher than a Busch race. There's much more media attention. You're trying to learn about these cars, get used to the extra 200 horsepower. There's a million things going on. It's hard to concentrate on all of them.

"I thought we'd miss a race or two. To miss the amount we did [eight] is pretty upsetting. With the exception of one race, maybe two, we'd have been in every race if it hadn't been for provisionals [starting spots awarded to established teams.]

"It's tough for people to compete who only have a $4 million or $5 million sponsor. It's tough enough when you have a veteran team and a rookie driver. A rookie team *and* a rookie driver is even tougher. I don't have a teammate. If you have a teammate, you have the notes from the other driver. When you get to the track, you have the basic information. But when we go to the track, we're learning the setup. If you can't unload at a Winston Cup race and be in the fine-tuning stages—where you just have to make minor changes before qualifying—you're in trouble. I want to be Winston Cup champion, but the first goal is to be in contention to win every race like Jeff Gordon, Mark Martin, and Dale Jarrett."

Jones was a rookie in another arena in 1999: He got married on December 19, 1998.

Opposite: Although it may appear that Buckshot Jones is strapped into a parachute, he's merely checking the safety equipment on his race car before he starts his engine.

"I've known my wife, Jina, since I was six. When I was 19, we started dating," says Jones, who admits to an adjustment period. "I can't stand my house being messy. The bathroom, kitchen—everything's got to be clean. I get so aggravated because she just lays stuff all over. I hate to see stuff piled up, and I'm a real fanatic about laundry. She'll let it build up until it's full, but not me."

Otherwise, Jones says that balancing marriage and career has been easy.

"She loves racing, goes to every race," he says. "If we get to a race early, we go sightseeing. I went to Pikes Peak and drove up, to the arch in St. Louis, to Hoover Dam in Las Vegas. Once we start practicing, my free time is in my coach watching TV—Westerns, older movies. The

best I eat is when I'm on the road and our bus driver, Carl Miles and Lindy, his wife, cook lunch and dinner. Free weekends, I go to our farm in Georgia, hunt and fish. I like spending time with my family, not just Mom, Dad, and my sister, but aunts and uncles. Family is the most important thing to me, and racing is second.

"My schedule is hectic because I do a lot of appearances," Jones adds. "That's part of the job. Some are fun, especially with kids-oriented charities. I admire kids who've got some disease, seeing how strong they are. They don't have long to live, but they're so happy."

Jones's primary focus when he gets to the track is earning a starting spot.

"It's shocked me to see how close everybody is in qualifying," he says. "Qualifying's when you get nervous. Atlanta draws hair on the back of your neck because it's *fast*. If your car's not exactly right, Darlington's nerve-wracking. If you don't make it the first day, everybody should have to requalify the second. You shouldn't be allowed to stand on your time. The temperature changes, the track changes, and there's many a time nobody's faster. Once you're in the field, you want to make at least 10- or 15-lap practice runs. Your car may start really loose, but after 15 laps, it may tighten up."

Jones is thankful for his moniker, which prevents confusion with one of the world's finest boxers.

"I hate being called Roy," he says. "I was two years old, tripped, and hit my head against a table. A knot on my head was getting bigger. I wanted to keep playing. My grandfather said, 'That boy's tough as buckshot.' The name stuck."

Although he weighs only 138 pounds, Jones chose activities that required him to be as "tough as buckshot."

"I played baseball, football, boxed Golden Gloves, showed horses, loved to barefoot ski," he recalls. "We used to ride motorcycles and go-karts on our farm. A friend started racing motocross, and I told Dad that's what I wanted. He said, 'Get in something that will protect you—a stock car.' We bought a car, went to Lanier Raceway. I spun three times. When I got out, I told Dad, 'This is what I want.' I was hooked."

"I was at the University of Georgia and had to maintain a 'B' average to keep racing," says Jones, who earned a degree in business management. "After probably the sixth race, Dad said, 'You could stay here and race, or we can have a game plan to get to Winston Cup.' From then on, whenever we'd get competitive in a series, we'd move to the next—late-model stocks to All-Pro to Busch. We've moved pretty quick. There've been times I was too aggressive."

Every step of the way, Jones's father, Billy, has been his car owner and mentor. "I'm on the phone with Dad five or six times a day," he says. "If I've got a question or problem, Dad has the answer. My mom got pregnant with my sister in '68, and Dad quit racing modifieds and started digging ditches. He worked from being a ditch digger to owning all these cable companies [under the banner of Fiber Optic, which has been a frequent sponsor of Buckshot's racing efforts]. Dad's my No. 1 supporter, but he's my No. 1 critic."

Former Busch Series champion Randy LaJoie, Jones's foil in one of racing's most celebrated rivalries of recent vintage, might argue that he's Buckshot's No. 1 critic.

"That started *before* we got to the track," Jones says. "My team, LaJoie's, and Elton Sawyer's were staying at the same Talladega motel, some dump. We were shooting bottle rockets at each other and playing around. I went to bed, and the alarm was going off on my Pontiac. I kept shutting it off with my remote. Finally, I walked out and said, 'Quit.' Five minutes later, I looked out, and LaJoie's beating his butt against my car. The next morning, Bob Sutton [then Sawyer's car owner] had jacked my car up on four jack stands. I started laughing. It was just a joke. But there was a big dent where Randy had been beating his butt against my car. I told a guy, 'Tell Randy he put a dent in the car. I'll send him the bill.' We go to the drivers' meeting, and Randy said, 'Everybody needs to be patient—a lot of give and take.' Eight laps into the deal, Randy hit me in the rear, spun me out, tore up a lot of cars. After the race, Randy said on TV, 'I got hit from behind, and I hit Buckshot.' The tape clearly shows nobody touched him. We went in the NASCAR trailer, and LaJoie said he never touched me. I said, 'You're a liar. Look at the back of my car. There's blue paint all over the bumper. I didn't paint the thing blue.' He said, 'I never touched you.' I said, 'You're a champion. Act like one.'

"We go to Indianapolis Raceway Park, and Randy ran a car off my bumper *in practice*. Then we go to Bristol, and Randy wrecked me again. So I tried to drill him during a caution period. But the rear end was so torn up, I missed. My worst moment was when I *didn't* hit him. I told Mike Helton [NASCAR's Vice President of Competition], 'We've told you we had problems, and you're not doing anything. What I did was wrong, but he deliberately wrecked me.'

"We went to Nazareth. Eight laps into the race, [LaJoie] hit Patty Moise, and I hit him and destroyed his car. We later raced against each other at New Hampshire harder than we've ever raced in our lives. You couldn't have fit a piece of paper between our cars, but we never touched. I got some respect from him that day, and he got it from me."

Jones calls his biggest thrill "my first Busch win at Milwaukee—pretty awesome," but he figures the best is yet to come.

"It's so much bigger to win a Winston Cup race," he says. "Winston Cup is the best—the cream of the crop. Even if you have the worst day racing, you can sign autographs after a race, and fans will pump you back up. It's neat to have people supporting you and get paid to do something you love, and I don't think Winston Cup racing has even come close to reaching its peak."

Following pages: **"Darlington's nerve-wracking,"** says Jones, who awaits a qualifying attempt at NASCAR's oldest superspeedway. The track's egg-shaped configuration puts a premium on handling and makes the setup difficult to optimize.

HANK JONES
Souvenir Sales

"A few years ago, some drivers thought there wasn't any money in souvenirs, called them trinkets and trash," says Hank Jones, President of Sports Design Inc., one of stock-car racing's premier souvenir enterprises. "We'd have a hat, a shirt, and a bumper sticker. Now, I have 151 items on Mark Martin alone."

Jones estimates the lion's share of drivers' incomes is now derived from "endorsements and souvenirs, especially superstars like Dale Earnhardt, Jeff Gordon, and Mark. The tracks, sponsors, drivers, and car owners realize now that souvenirs are a big deal. I represented Dale from 1984 to 1994. In those days, the driver basically got it all. Now, you pay an average of 20 percent to drivers and teams. Some sponsors are probably making more than they're putting in because of souvenirs. I don't know if it's a $2 billion-a-year business or whatever, but I know sales have skyrocketed.

"Along with higher sales have come higher costs. We've got a portable store we bring to races at a very high cost. The bigger companies are hard to compete with. What makes my job difficult is the size of my company and still remaining independent—totally owned by my family and myself. My piece of the world is not as big as it was in '92, '93, and '94, but I'm much happier."

Jones's road to transforming "trinkets and trash" into a king's ransom was not without its share of potholes.

Opposite: **When Rusty Wallace (whose back is to the camera) won the Winston Cup championship in 1989, Hank Jones was selling his souvenirs. The two have remained close friends. Benny Ertel is on the left.**

"I was engraving sunglasses in Gatlinburg, Tennessee. I started on the sidewalk. It took me 15 years to save enough to get a shop," he recalls. "About 1980, I started going to tracks. The tracks wanted nothing to do with the souvenir business. Everybody was down the street somewhere. I had a Blazer with a fold-out table and a portable engraving machine. I'd find a spot on the grass and was making quite a living selling engraved sunglasses. I met Bobby Allison, a great guy, and talked to him about souvenirs. I thought there was a market that wasn't being fulfilled, and I started visualizing the future in the souvenir business. We set up our little deal beside my engraved sunglasses. Bobby signed autographs and got me inside the track. I thought I was on cloud nine."

Jones's crusade to move his trailers to the convenient trackside locations that now house scores of such rigs may have been the most significant landmark in the growth of racing's souvenir business.

"We were out in fields," he says. "We had a beautiful Miller American trailer with Bobby, and we had Dale. Our rigs looked nice and clean. I was telling the others, 'Get a nice-looking trailer. Let's look professional and go trackside.' My mother and father and God gave me the gift to visualize what I wanted, and I was able to relay that to the drivers. I saw we could make it work. I started knocking on doors. I was pretty pushy, overly aggressive sometimes. Track owners would ask the driver to do them a favor, and the driver would say, 'Our souvenir trailer's sitting across the street. Let us bring it over.'

"[Former Martinsville Speedway owner] Clay Earles turned me down three or four times. I think he got tired of seeing me coming, so he finally said, 'Set one trailer up, and see what you do.' Everybody else was two or three miles from the track. I had a really good week. I thanked him, and he saw it wasn't detrimental. In Atlanta, Walt Nix was the owner. I tried several times to get an interview, but he wouldn't have anything to do with me. One day I saw this old gentleman across the street in the cow pasture mowing grass. I got him to stop the mower and told him I was selling souvenirs, looking for a place to set up trailers. I told him I'd pay, and he said, 'OK.' I said, 'How do I get in touch with you?' He handed me a card, and it was Walt Nix. I almost dropped in my shoes. We were in that field for several years and finally graduated to the track. The biggest turnaround was Daytona. We were along Airport Road, always trying to get closer to the track. There was a little strip where the track parked campers for $25 apiece. Bill France Jr. finally turned that over to us, and it's probably bringing him at least $1 million per race now."

Jones's battle for acceptance reached full cycle in 1997, when he received the Humpy Wheeler Award, "which is very special, because it's awarded for promoting racing. It's probably my most prized possession."

Jones's 11-year tenure with Earnhardt pro-

Opposite top: Jones (foreground) provides the motorhome, and Ertel (background) does the cooking when they're at the track. Jones calls Ertel's cooking "so good it will make you want to slap your Grandma." Opposite bottom: Jones observes the Roush Racing crew as it prepares Mark Martin's car at Darlington. Jones often has been a member of the pit crew on Martin's Busch Series car.

duced one of stock-car racing's most famous nicknames. "Dale didn't even have a trailer before then. The first year, we called Dale the Dominator," Jones recalls. "But I came up with the Intimidator, because that's the way I've always seen Dale. He's intimidating on and off the track, but not if you really know him."

Jones, who formed Sports Design after he sold Sports Image to Earnhardt in 1994, "resents anybody taking credit for making Dale a millionaire or making Dale who he is except Dale.

Souvenir success was based on his performance. The things he did on the track made it easy for me off the track.

"I think Dale had told Mark I'd done a good job when Mark and I got together in 1995," Jones adds. "I don't think a week goes by that Mark doesn't say, 'You're doing a good job.' But Mark's got a great fan base. Mark's the most believable spokesperson [A 1999 credibility study by *IEG Endorsement Insider* had Martin tied for first place with Bill Cosby]. That's the kind of guy Mark is.

"I wish somebody could follow Mark for one month and see just how little home time he has. Along with these endorsements come hours and hours of autograph sessions for sponsors. You can't ask which day they've got free next week. You've got to ask which day they've got over the next three months. I had Rusty Wallace's souvenirs in 1989, when he was champion. Rusty—a true friend, the one guy in my life that anything Hank wanted, I got—is gone *every day*."

Not only have Winston Cup facilities made souvenir rigs easily accessible, but Jones says another important addition is that most tracks now provide motorhome campgrounds for racing personnel.

"Until a few years ago, it was impossible to have your wife and family at the track," he says. "I saw them sitting in vans all day on 100-degree days. Now, the tracks have these facilities for the drivers so their families can come.

"I go to virtually all the races. I have a motorcoach. Benny [Ertel, Martin's business manager] and I spend a lot of time together. Chef Benny does all the cooking. My office hours are basically whenever the track's open. My time in the garage, talking to sponsors, drivers, and teams, is very valuable. I love that I can walk five feet, shake somebody's hand, and there's another friend standing another five feet away. I wouldn't take anything in the world for the people I've met in racing, like Neil Bonnett. Other than Benny, the best friend I've ever had was Neil. I always said, 'If Neil doesn't like you, you need to take a real good look at yourself.' When Neil got killed [on February 13, 1994, while practicing for the Daytona 500], that was the most devastating time of my life.

"I enjoy what I'm doing, and as long as I enjoy seeing all those people, I'm going to continue," Jones adds. "I'm almost a stranger at home. My wife has basically raised our family. Every day that goes by, I appreciate my family more. Money and material things aren't substitutes. I'm trying to find more time for my family."

But that doesn't mean he'll forego his hobby—racing Legends cars. "I've never been any good, but I've had a great time," he says. "I'm in the Masters. Somebody asked, 'Is that for old folks?' I said, 'No, that's for Masters—guys who know what they're doing.' At least that's my story."

DEAN KESSEL
Manager of Sports Marketing for Lowe's Companies

When Dean Kessel, Manager of Sports Marketing for Lowe's Companies, was a young-ster sitting in the Charlotte Motor Speedway grandstand, he never imagined he'd someday broker a groundbreaking, $35 million deal with the facility.

"My father was a race fan. I wasn't," Kessel recalls. "I would sit in the grandstand, put the headset on, and listen to a football game.

"I always wanted to be in sports marketing, not necessarily in racing. I did an internship with R.J. Reynolds. [The late] T. Wayne Robertson, who was President of [RJR's] Sports Mar-keting Enterprises, said they get hundreds of resumes, and 95 percent say, 'I'm a big fan. I'd love to work in the sport.' It's the wrong thing to say. When I interview people for a job, if they say they're fans, it kind of cuts them out of the equation. When you're at the track, you represent the company. If you're a big fan, you're just not going to focus on the task at hand. If you're asking for autographs, you lose credibility with the people you have to see.

"In 1994, RJR's sports marketing division was looking at doing outside business, and one of their first clients was Lowe's. I was doing research as an intern and got to know the Lowe's people. Wayne told them we were going to assign some top-line people who know this sport. And Dale Pond, Lowe's Executive Vice President of marketing and merchandising, said, 'We want Dean.' Wayne said, 'We haven't even offered him a job.' Dale said, 'We've been work-ing with him for six or eight months, and we like him.' So Wayne said, 'You've got him.' I got hired in the middle of a meeting.

"After the meeting, I walked into Wayne's office and said, 'I hope they didn't put you in an awkward position.' He said, 'We were going to hire you. We just weren't sure where we were going to put you.' That was a great moment in my career. T. Wayne and Jeff Byrd, the Vice President of SME who is now Vice President and General Manager of Bristol Motor Speed-way, were unbelievably creative. One thing that impressed me about Wayne is he was com-fortable with both the jackman in the garage and the executives in the boardroom.

"I was on the Lowe's account for SME, running the public relations, marketing, and show car for three years. Lowe's decided to create a sports marketing division and asked me to head that. Dale was instrumental in getting me to come over.

"I'm married, and we have three little boys to keep us busy, so I'm fortunate I don't have to travel as much as I used to. I wear a lot of hats, trying to handle ticket and credential requests, recommendations about sponsorships, a lot of meetings, a lot of planning. I'm also responsible for our relationship with NFL teams, NBA teams, and major-league baseball.

"It's not a mundane job. There's always something you can do that may help drive customers into the store. Because of all the things we're doing and the direction we're going, I've never felt I'd lose my job."

Lowe's most visible ventures in Winston Cup racing are the Richard Childress-owned Chevrolet driven by Mike Skinner and the title sponsorship of the track founded in 1960 as Charlotte Motor Speedway.

The latter venture, the first of its kind in motorsports, was the crowning moment of Kessel's burgeoning career. But it quickly involved the worst. In the first extravaganza under the Lowe's Motor Speedway banner, three spectators were killed at an Indy Racing League event on May 1, 1999.

"It was horrific—a tragedy that had never happened in the 40 years of this speedway," says Kessel, who served as Lowe's spokesperson about the calamity. "Certainly, from a corporate standpoint, that's not the way you want to start a relationship. There are some inherent risks involved with motorsports. But I'm very proud of the professionalism with which it was handled. [Lowe's Motor Speedway employees] were a class act. It probably made us closer to the people we work with. We now know how they react. They know how we react.

"The Lowe's Motor Speedway deal—a $35 million commitment—is something positive in my career. We're signed with Richard Childress through 2002. We've got a 10-year commitment through 2009 with Lowe's Motor Speedway. It was a perfect match for us. Our corporate offices in North Wilkesboro are an hour and a half away. Speedway Motorsports Incorporated has been a leader in the industry—the first to have suites, condominiums, a speedway club. We had the opportunity to get any SMI track, and Charlotte's the crown jewel—the premier facility, we believe, on the circuit.

Opposite: **Larry McReynolds, crew chief for the Lowe's Chevrolet, discusses the team's outlook with Dean Kessel (right), who represents Lowe's investment in sports.**

"It's part of trying to differentiate yourself from your competition in getting your message out. What can you do from a sponsorship viewpoint that's different, touches a different segment of the market? We try to think forward to what fans' reactions will be to our actions. You've got to be very particular on how you go to market, who you choose to drive your car, to represent you. The bottom line is you've got to be able to measure it back to sales.

"When the Chevrolet goes around the track, it has Lowe's on the hood. If you could put your logo on the Dallas Cowboys—take the star off and put your logo on—you would. That type thing has been going on in motorsports for decades. Fans are receptive to it. They realize the sport wouldn't exist without sponsors. I get letters every week that say, 'Thank you for sponsoring my favorite sport.' The growth of the sport is phenomenal. This is a great marketing tool for us. We know it's working."

BOBBY LABONTE
Winston Cup Driver

In his first five years of driving Joe Gibbs's Interstate Batteries Pontiac, Bobby Labonte won 12 Winston Cup races, 17 poles, and became a star. When Gibbs hired him before the 1995 season, however, Labonte's career was in jeopardy.

"I couldn't sleep at night or get up in the morning. I couldn't physically get out of bed before noon a lot of days," Labonte recalls. "I went from 170 to 148 pounds. My heartbeat was 120 beats a minute. I thought it was from stress and worrying."

On December 26, 1994, Labonte learned his problem was Graves' disease, a thyroid disorder that causes enlargement of the gland, overproduction of the hormone produced by the thyroid, and abnormal protrusion of the eyeballs.

"The doctor said I'd probably had the disease for six months," he recalls. "Another doctor told me I wouldn't race for six months. I went to the Mayo Clinic, and they said, 'We'll put you on medicine. Come back in two weeks, and we'll give you radiation and kill the thyroid.' No guarantees I'd drive. Your eyesight could go bad. You're vulnerable to a stroke at any time. I canceled all my appearances, didn't do anything until the Daytona 500. I got back to normal, but I'll take medicine every day for the rest of my life."

Unlike 1994, when David Green won the Busch Series title for a team owned by Labonte, normal now means Bobby figures to challenge for the Winston Cup championship every year.

"I've won a Busch championship. If I win a Winston Cup championship, that would put me in a category nobody's achieved in the modern era," he says. "But that's not the goal. It's more than I would have dreamed to be competitive enough to *have a chance* to win a championship every year. All you can ask for is an opportunity to win a championship. Today, I've got that. I don't ever want to be *too* comfortable, but I don't want somebody with an axe over my head."

Labonte obviously isn't particularly concerned about losing his ride with Gibbs, because few drivers more readily accept the blame for on-track altercations.

"If I'm responsible, I'll take the blame. If you think you're wrong, say you're wrong. I'm not

going to say I didn't do it," says Labonte, who points to an accident he caused, not an injury he suffered or a narrow defeat, as his worst experience in racing. "My worst moment is throwing my helmet at my car at Bristol. I drove right into John Andretti. I wasn't paying attention. I was talking on the radio and should have been listening to the spotter. I was mad.

"I broke my shoulder the week before the [1999] race at Texas. After the race, I was *hurting*, tired, cold. My neck was sore. Somebody said, 'That sure is heroic.' I thought, 'That wasn't heroic, because a friend of ours has leukemia. He's in the hospital, his hair's falling out, and he's got stuff flowing through his body all the time.' If you can do that and still want to live, that's a hero."

Labonte attributes his success to "driving talent, understanding a race car, being Terry's brother, and being in the right place at the right time." He began racing quarter-midgets in his native Corpus Christi, Tex., at age five, then drove "very sporadically—mostly go-karts."

"When Terry started driving stock cars, I became Terry's No. 1 fan. We'd travel like *The Beverly Hillbillies*," he adds. "We had a motorhome we'd sleep in, 10 or 12 of us. Terry met Billy Hagan, so we moved to North Carolina. I went to work for Hagan Racing, basically sweeping floors. Eddie Dickerson and Gary DeHart let me work on cars. [Crew chief] Jake Elder thought I wasn't old enough. The only thing Jake would let me do was go to the bank to get dollar bills to play poker."

When Dale Inman became Terry's crew chief, Bobby began "taking care of parts, fabricating, welding, putting cars together, taking cars apart. I still washed the van and swept the floor, but the other things I *loved*, because I was learning a lot. When Terry left to drive for Junior Johnson [in 1987], they fired my dad and told me to leave, too."

Labonte says he then received "the best advice I ever had," when Terry told him to buy a race car and compete at Caraway Speedway in nearby Asheboro, where he won the 1987 track championship.

"My dad was instrumental in helping me," he says.

> **Opposite top:** Labonte believes that "understanding a race car" is one of his primary assets as a driver. He performed many mechanical tasks in his early racing days and once owned a Busch Series championship team. **Opposite bottom:** At Daytona at the beginning of the 1999 season, Labonte and his Joe Gibbs crew get accustomed to being a two-car team. A second car, sponsored by Home Depot, was added for Tony Stewart, who earned the 1999 Rookie of the Year award.

"Terry pointed me in the right direction. Instead of the blind leading the blind, he was definitely the smart one leading the blind. I ran Busch full time in 1990, won the championship in '91, and finished second by *three points* in '92 behind Joe Nemechek. Bill Davis gave me the chance in Winston Cup in '93 with a rookie team. I went to the shop every day, worked on cars—hard work, but fun. When Joe bought my contract in '95, that was very instrumental, and [crew chief] Jimmy Makar has been instrumental for the blood, sweat, and tears that go into this."

Labonte no longer labors in the shop, but now has other demands on his time.

"Tuesday, I go to the shop, talk to Jimmy, all the guys," he says. "Wednesday, half a day is probably personal; half is doing interviews or signing autographs. There are days like Thursday: I've got to be in Michigan at 10 a.m. for an appearance. The following week, I've got to be in San Francisco at 9 a.m. Wednesday for an appearance. I had to be at Dover Thursday morning at 7:45 for MBNA. If the sponsors think I'm representing them well, I'm just doing what I've been taught by my parents—be yourself, be honest, work hard, and don't be a jerk.

"If somebody asks you for your autograph, you might as well be ready. Instead of complaining, carry a Sharpie. I went to Vail, Colorado, and got noticed. It comes with the territory. Today, a lady had a poster of The Winston with her at the mall. I don't know if she carries it all the time, but she had it with her. It's harder to lead a normal life, but the benefits are worth the effort."

And Labonte makes every effort to lead a normal life.

"I play computer games, video games, play with the kids," he says. "We swim in the summer. I'm not Tim Allen, but I'll paint a wall, little things like that.

"With the motorhome, we're able to take the kids to races. We watch movies in the motorhome. Each weekend's different. It's kind of cool. My wife might bring Tyler, Madison, or both. She might not come until Saturday and not bring either one. If she's there, she does the cooking. Sometimes we'll go out to eat, or Terry and I will see what food we've got in our motorhomes. I'll cook steak, shrimp, or chicken on the grill. I'll fix a salad, macaroni & cheese, beans, potatoes. Ham and cheese sandwiches are great. I can eat frozen dinners with the best of them.

"Donna doesn't go every weekend. She thinks there's more to life than racing, especially as far as our kids are concerned. They need a well-balanced life and not just, 'Daddy, why don't we live in a motorhome all the time? Why do we sit in the back of the van when we leave the track? Why are there always 45 people fixing to beat the window in?' "

When Labonte has similar questions about life's problems, he turns to Donna.

"I can ask Terry anything any time, yet I won't ask him everything all the time," he says. "If it's something really deep, I always go to my wife. She might not tell me what I want to hear, which is good, because I can ask a lot of people things, and they'll tell me what I want to hear, and sometimes that's not right. She's important, and Terry's important, too. My best moment was 1996 in Atlanta—a special day for our family because Terry won his second championship and I won the race."

Opposite: **After his victory in the 1999 Pennsylvania 500 at Pocono, Labonte gets a congratulatory hug from his son, Tyler.**

If Labonte ruled NASCAR, he'd make it illegal for teams to field more than two cars. "It isn't healthy for the sport," he says.

What he does consider a bonanza for the sport is the nationwide expansion into larger markets that Winston Cup racing is continuing to experience.

"Building tracks in Texas, California, Kansas City, Chicago, New York, New Hampshire, and Miami is an inspiration," he says. "But the best thing NASCAR ever did was have an annual credential. I went from Busch to Cup, got my annual, and thought I owned the world."

JULIET MACUR
Motorsports Journalist

Lest anyone think Juliet Macur is "a fan who gets to walk around the garage," she'll set the record straight.

"I was picking up a credential, and people were in line to park cars or work in concessions," says Macur, who earned both her bachelor's and master's degrees at New York's prestigious Columbia School of Journalism before she became *The Orlando Sentinel's* motorsports reporter. "I remember going through this door just for the press, and this guy said, 'The press gets everything, and all they do is watch races. It's so easy. We have the hard jobs.' I was so mad. I was thinking, 'What are you talking about?'

"There's a lot of pressure filing on time for a night race. It's pretty humiliating to put together a story and have the whole world read it. What if you misspell some guy's name or have Richard Petty winning 250 races? There's a lot of pressure when you know there are readers who know NASCAR very well, look for every fact, and are the first to call if you're wrong."

Although many of her readers have followed Winston Cup racing far longer than Macur, she's determined to eliminate such criticism.

"I'm learning so much about the sport," she says. "I want to get a job done. I've always been really intense. You get to bed at 11 p.m., and you've got to wake up at 4. I like to be in the garage when it opens. If I was a crew member, I'd want to see the journalists out there in the morning. When some of them stroll in at 11 a.m. or noon, it's sort of embarrassing. It's a sense of pride that I'm the first there and the last to leave. It's the way I've always been. It's an energy factor. I was training for the Olympics in rowing, so for several years I was completely obsessed with that. I'll never become mellow no matter how many times people say, 'Chill out. You need to relax.' It's part of my personality.

Opposite: Juliet Macur interviews crew chief Larry McReynolds in 1999 with reporter Barry Svrluga. After graduating from Columbia, Macur went to work at *The Orlando Sentinel* as its motorsports reporter.

"My editor, Lynn Hoppes, is very energetic, has a lot of great ideas, and knows how to push me in the right direction. I think I'm a better reporter than writer right now. I think I'm going through the right evolution, being a really strong reporter, and learning how to craft as

I go along. What I enjoy most is telling a really long story and talking to 100 people about it. It's tough when you're turning out stuff every day, not writing those big pieces because there's no time. But I love reporting, talking to people.

"When I was an intern, they sent me to the 1997 Pepsi 400 at Daytona. The two other writers thought it was great that the young reporter was really excited about being there. Two months after the Pepsi 400, the NASCAR job came open. Not many people at the paper wanted to cover NASCAR because of the traveling and long days. I'd talked so much about the Pepsi 400, how intriguing it was, and how interesting the personalities were, that my boss put me on that beat. I had a dean at Columbia named Sandy Padwe. He pushed me in the sports direction. He encouraged me that NASCAR would be a good beat, a good opportunity, when they offered me the job. It's a great job for someone who wanted to cover a pro beat. My dad was a mechanic, so it's not that strange I'm covering racing. We used to go to short-track races in New Jersey, but I never thought I'd be there every week. My former classmates are covering things like high school wrestling, so I've got one up on them.

"People don't realize how big a business NASCAR really is. Winston Cup is filled with good stories and great history. There are a lot of thrills in this sport, and the fans are great. I really admire the drivers. People put their lives on the line when they get in the car. You never know what's going to happen. You have 43 drivers in the race, so there's always a good story. There's never a weekend where you have nothing going on, which is great. I cover pro football, too, and the people in racing are incredibly accessible, more willing to talk, compared to other professional athletes.

"I like the younger drivers, the Dale Earnhardt Juniors, the Elliott Sadlers. I don't think they've been distorted by the pressure yet. Ask Dale Jr. an offbeat question, and you get a huge offbeat answer that I love. Elliott is hilarious. It'll be nice to follow their careers to see if they end up being like the cranky old guys.

"Who wants to talk to somebody who's cranky, anyway? They might bite your head off. You don't go up to Mark Martin or Dale Earnhardt when they're in a bad mood. I was a little embarrassed when Earnhardt won the 125-miler in the first race I covered and grabbed my credential in front of everybody to see who I was. He said, 'I didn't think I'd seen you before. What's your name?' He scared the daylights out of me. I know now that's just him, but I was freaking out! The first time I covered a race, the two other reporters sent me out after Martin after he crashed in a last-lap shootout. I was determined to get a quote. He bit my head off. It was awful.

"But I really admire Mark for his intensity. He's so focused and doesn't care what you think of him. People criticize him for being cranky, too focused, or not positive enough, but he gets the job done. It's admirable to be so focused on something and not let anything get in your way.

"I admire my parents the most," Macur adds. "During World War II, my mother was sent to a work camp and my father to a concentration camp. We're Catholic, but they lived in Poland. The Nazis burned down everyone's house, killed their farm animals, put everyone on trains, and shipped them away. My dad was in Dachau, one of the worst. His older brother was killed as part of the Polish underground."

Macur admits her intense desire to succeed in journalism dominates her life.

"There isn't time to have a normal life," she says. "I get home from races on Monday. We have a motorsports page on Thursday, so I try to wake up at 6 a.m. Tuesday. During football season, I cover the Jaguars on Tuesday and write the motorsports page at the same time. I'm home for two days a week. I try to do laundry, take everything to the cleaners, get my hair cut, go to the doctor. On Thursday morning, I leave for a race. I hang out in my hotel room, transcribe tapes. Most of the time, I don't eat dinner. I feel guilty if I have free time. That means I'm not working hard enough.

"I really question how people in racing have relationships. It's not likely I'd meet somebody where I live, in Flagler Beach, anyway. I'd be marrying somebody who's 101.

"When I'm home, I either go to the gym or the beach. It's really difficult to keep in shape—as you may notice if you look around the media center. I try to avoid the food in the media center. I have a bit of an ethical problem with the media waiting for lunch. At a race the other day, people were like, 'We're going to starve because the race is starting, and they haven't fed us.' Everybody was complaining, and I said, 'Go get your own lunch.' I don't think the media deserve anything, like free hats or shirts. That's where sportswriters get bad raps. My goal in becoming a sportswriter is to make it more news-oriented, more respected, and not have people thinking you're getting a free lunch or autographs. I see media asking for autographs after interviews. It's embarrassing. If you're really passionate about being a journalist, writing the truth, it's ridiculous to have Dale Earnhardt sign your T-shirt."

Macur prefers a token of appreciation.

"One driver said after I wrote a story on him, 'That really did justice to our team.' That was a high point," she says. "With all the things drivers are thinking about and all the people they have to deal with—owners, crews, sponsors, and media—for them to go out of their way and say one nice thing is nice. You don't hear many nice things—ever. And you have to appreciate getting access to people. Once I was sitting with Earnhardt in his trailer. When I walked out and all the local media and fans were there, I thought, 'Wow! I feel really lucky to do something other people would kill to do, even though I'm not awestruck by it.' You really have to think how lucky you are once in a while and not complain about the hours or pressure. It *is* a fun job. It could be worse. You could be an accountant."

LARRY McREYNOLDS
Crew Chief

His 23 Winston Cup victories confirm Larry McReynolds's stature as one of racing's best crew chiefs—which means he's more Bear Bryant than Mr. Goodwrench.

"It's no different than a football coach," says McReynolds, overseer of the Lowe's Chevrolet, driven by Mike Skinner, for Richard Childress Racing. *"You've got to be a good leader and manager.* Being a great mechanic has become a small part. It's orchestrating, moving the pieces. The hours are tough. For every ounce of glory, there's *gallons* of blood, sweat, and tears. Travel, being away from family, is tough. The frustrating thing is so many things are out of your control—a flat tire, somebody spinning in front of you. But the toughest part is people. You've got so many different personalities, needs, and wants."

McReynolds says successful crew chiefs "never quit thinking about this sport. If you work 20 hours a day, somebody's going to work 21. You work 24, somebody's going to figure out how to work 26. You crawl in that airplane after the race, dig the briefcase out, and look at what you've got coming up."

McReynolds creatively finds time for his wife and three children.

"I'm the fast-food king. There probably isn't a meter that can measure my cholesterol," he says. "I don't know who created a lunch *hour.* If I can eat in 20 minutes and work for 40, that *might* be 40 minutes I can spend with my family. If I leave at 6 o'clock, I'm able to have dinner with Linda and the kids and maybe watch a movie. But once the kids go to bed, I go in the office in my home, look over notes, do paperwork.

"The greatest thing we've done is buy a motorcoach. It gives them a home at the track. We spend more quality time at the track than at home. Linda knew what she got into when she met me, and it takes a special wife to put up with this. She understands. The wives who don't, you'll see a ring on a guy's finger for a couple of years. All of a sudden, the ring'll be gone. It's like, 'My wife couldn't take it anymore.' "

Then why continue?

"Racing has been awesome to us. We've put a ton into it, but it's given us a good living," he says. "The money is good—and getting better—for drivers, crew chiefs, tire changers, engine builders. If you'd told me *five* years ago crew chiefs would be making the money they're making, I'd have said, 'Is that in a *total* of five years?'"

> **Opposite:** With a stack of worn tires serving as a tabletop for his clipboard, Larry McReynolds times Mike Skinner at Richmond. The efficacy of small adjustments to the setup can be judged immediately with his stopwatch.

"Racing is like a disease. It gets in your bloodstream. What drives me is matching wits with the greatest crew chiefs in the business—the Ray Evernhams, Jimmy Makars, Robin Pembertons, Todd Parrotts. I thrive on trying to win every practice, qualifying session, race. *Every* win is great, but the best were the first Winston Cup win with Ricky Rudd at Watkins Glen in 1988, the [1992] Daytona 500 with Davey [Allison], the [1998] Daytona 500 with Dale Earnhardt, and leading 328 of 334 laps in the 500-miler at Charlotte in '93 with Ernie [Irvan]."

McReynolds never envisioned such triumphs when he was a volunteer crew member for his aunt, Noreen Mears, who raced in the street-stock division in his native Birmingham.

"My aunt said, 'I can do that.' Her husband, Butch, laughed and said, 'Drum up enough sponsorship. We'll see if you really want it.' She drummed up about as many sponsors as you could put on one car," McReynolds recalls. "We built her a '65 Chevrolet Caprice. Butch, a good mechanic who taught me a lot, got me a job at Charles Finley Auto Parts, which was pretty scary because I didn't know a brake rotor from a windshield. That's how little mechanical inclination I had. My senior year in high school [1977], I'd go to school four hours, work at that salvage yard, then work on race cars.

"People ask me, 'How do I get in Winston Cup?' I say, 'Find a local racer who's going to work your tail off all hours of the night. It's probably going to *cost* you money. You're going to make your family mad because you're working on race cars every night. If you can make it through that, it gets easier.' "

It didn't for McReynolds, who moved to Winston Cup racing when he answered an advertisement in the *NASCAR Newsletter* about a team being formed in Greenville, S.C., by Bob Rogers. "I hung the phone up and said, 'I was probably one of 10 million calls.' Two weeks later, Dana Williamson, Bob's daughter, said, 'We'd *love* for you to work for us.' We ran 30 of 31 races in 1981. There were three full-time employees. It was seven days a week. We maybe got Christmas Day off, Thanksgiving if we were lucky. You drove everywhere. Today, a guy complains if he has to ride on a King Air to Fort Worth," he says.

When Rogers's team folded in 1982, McReynolds was approached by Mark Martin's mother, Jackie, who was managing her son's rookie campaign. "She said, 'Would you be the crew chief?' I said, 'I'm not ready. I haven't been in the business *two* years.' She said, 'We want to give you that title.' That was my first official title," he says.

When Martin's operation folded, McReynolds rejoined Rogers upon the latter's return to racing. A couple of races later, McReynolds recalls, "Bob said, 'Baby Boy, which is what he called me, I'm done.' "

A stint with David Pearson ended when Pearson took the sponsorship to another team. Owner Bobby Hawkins then hired Butch Lindley as the driver.

"Butch went to Bradenton, Florida [for a short-track race]," McReynolds recalls. "The first phone call I got that Saturday night said he'd been killed. As it turned out, he wasn't killed, but he was in a coma. I'd watched three teams close, one take a sponsor somewhere else, and now a good friend is severely hurt. He passed away five years later.

"I thought that maybe racing isn't what it's supposed to be. The worst times of my career were getting a phone call that Davey was probably not going to survive the helicopter crash, getting the call on Butch, and witnessing Ernie's situation [a life-threatening crash at Michigan in 1994].

"Bobby ended up selling to Kenny Bernstein," McReynolds adds. "The '86 season was my first as crew chief of a full-fledged Winston Cup team. I'll always be grateful for Kenny taking a chance on me and teaching me about life, business, dealing with people, and communicating."

Late in 1989, McReynolds accepted a job with Robert Yates Racing, then had a change of heart. "I went back to the hotel and cried my eyes out," he recalls. "I said, 'I can't leave.' Linda said, 'You need to tell Robert.' We went to Atlanta and tested. I drove across the street to the pay phone to call Robert. I said, 'You'll probably hate my guts for the rest of my life, but I can't take that job. I've been with this 26 car even before it was born and can't just walk away.' He said, 'Larry, been there, done that. You've got all the respect in the world out of me.' "

Yates proved true to his word in 1991, when he hired McReynolds, who enjoyed a six-year, 19-victory tenure with Yates before he left for the chance to become Earnhardt's crew chief in 1997.

"If I've got heroes, they're Robert and Richard, two owners who've been very successful, done a lot for this sport, and worked their guts out. But when I took the job with Richard, I said, 'I won't promise you wins, and I sure won't be dumb enough to promise you a championship,' " says McReynolds, who won only once in 45 starts with Earnhardt before Childress switched his teams' crew chiefs. "There were so many things written: Dale and Larry hate each other, don't even agree the sun's bright, or the sky's blue. It wasn't any of those. My style and his style just wasn't a good match."

McReynolds doubles as a commentator for The Nashville Network, which has helped him watch racing more objectively.

"I *enjoy* TV very much," he says. "It's let me look at our sport through totally different eyes. The best change has been [Winston Cup Series Director] Gary Nelson cleaning it up, even though every time they make a rule change, we go ballistic. There's no suspicion now of big engines, light cars, low cars. Everything's out in the open."

McReynolds also advocates a change in perception.

"Ask your avid sports fans, 'Who won the World Series in 1998?' They'd say, 'The Yankees.' Who won the NBA championship? 'The Bulls.' Who won the Winston Cup championship? 'Jeff Gordon.' Wow! He's pretty phenomenal," McReynolds says. "He drove that car, built those motors, fixed those wrecks. I'm not degrading drivers, but I'd like to see guys who work 80-hour weeks, don't get to take their families to races, don't have motorcoaches, airplanes, boats, and houses in every climate in America, get recognition. It's a *team* sport—unless the driver gets out and changes tires on his own."

MORRIS METCALFE
NASCAR Chief Scorer

"I love numbers. They're second nature to me," says Morris Metcalfe. "I'm obsessed with scoring."

That obsession led to Metcalfe becoming NASCAR's chief scorer, a position he'll vacate in 2000.

"When I started, you did it for love of the sport," he says. "You got addicted. In 1951, I heard about this stock-car race in Darlington, South Carolina. I bought tickets—$6. The most expensive were the first four rows at $10 apiece. Harold Brasington, who built the track, put the most expensive seats, with back rests, down front—so close you couldn't see.

"The next February, I graduated from the University of Miami. I accepted a job with Western Electric in Winston-Salem, where they had a short-track race. They got people out of the grandstand and gave your money back if you scored a car. It was $2 to get in. So I got $2 for myself and $2 for my wife. I thought that was a pretty good deal, so I started going to races. I scored Tim Flock in '52, and Tim won the championship. Johnny Bruner Sr., the field manager for NASCAR—the only paid employee—hired me part-time in '53."

Metcalfe started as "a minor scoring official" for races at Piedmont Interstate Fairgrounds in Spartanburg, S.C., and North Carolina's Asheville-Weaverville Speedway. "Johnny gave me $15 for the two races," he recalls. "I thought I had a license to steal, because I was making less than $20 a day as an engineer. Two years later, [predecessor] Joe Epton—who stood up for me quite a few times—had me score races he couldn't. I scored my first race at the old three-quarter-mile dirt Charlotte Speedway.

Opposite: **Improvements in NASCAR's scoring system made by Morris Metcalfe have made once-common scoring disputes virtually non-existent.**

"I even did Broad Slab Speedway in Benson, North Carolina. We didn't have power, so we had a generator. The generator didn't have a governor, and I was trying to run a timer. The first guy would go out, and he'd be 28 seconds. The next guy'd be 41 seconds. The next guy would be 35. We found out a generator without a governor is not a good source of power. I went to Spring Lake, North Carolina, in 1953. The seats there went from tree stump to tree stump. They had boards, and the boards weren't in a row. They went wherever the stumps were. A race in Houston was the first time I rode in an air-conditioned

car, a 1956 Buick. I thought, 'Boy! This is living!' I stayed in the finest hotel in Houston. Cost me $8. Two years ago, one track on the Eastern Seaboard wanted a four-night minimum at $200 a night. One race, I went out, and Tiny Lund said, 'Don't leave. We borrowed a part off your car.' I had a brand-new '56 Ford station wagon, and he'd borrowed the air cleaner. He brought back the dirtiest thing. He later bought me a new one."

During those pioneer days, scoring disputes were nearly as common as flat tires.

"Some of those sessions, you'd go for three hours after a race," he recalls. "You'd have a driver and crew chief lay a pistol on the table and say, 'This is going to do my talking.' When they announced Johnny Beauchamp won the 1959 Daytona 500, I was pretty ill, to say the least. I knew Lee Petty had won. Big Bill [France] got the picture that gave irrefutable evidence Petty had won, and that made me feel a lot better, because I knew that was what I'd seen.

"I worked races until April of '82. [Former NASCAR Competition Director] Bill Gazaway heard I'd retired as an engineer. He flew me to Daytona Beach, threw me car keys, and said, 'Here's your ride home. The car is yours to use if you work for us [as chief scorer]. If you don't, we'll drop you off at the bus station.' Bill was very straightforward, rubbed some people wrong, but I worked extremely well with him."

Because of the scoring systems Metcalfe has implemented, today's rare scoring disputes come from fans who are "a little inebriated."

"At New Hampshire, Dover, and Charlotte, the scoring stand is in the fourth turn, not the start/finish line. I've had people call after a race to solve an argument," he says. "They say, 'The newspaper said so-and-so led the first lap, but I was at the start/finish line, and I *know* somebody else led.' I say, 'The scoring line is where we score, and that's in the fourth turn. The start/finish line is only for the end of the race.'

"We didn't go to modern scoring until 1991," he adds. "We've got three systems now, from 60 to 94 employees [depending on the track]. We have the system with scorecards—an update every 10 laps. After we had a problem picking up the correct leader at North Wilkesboro in 1990 in a race Brett Bodine won, we went to the button system with the computer. The button system updates scoring every lap. In '96, we went to the ANB transponder, which is about the size of a pack of cigarettes and bracketed to the fuel cell. Each time it crosses the scoring line, it sends a signal. That signal is distributed to radio, TV, race control, everywhere. People ask me, 'Why do you need three scoring systems?' I'll ask, 'How many times have you gone to your ATM and it wasn't working?' They'll say, 'About once every 10 times.' I'll say, 'We can't afford for a computer to go down once.'

"Recognition by NASCAR and the tracks that they needed better facilities to score and, in the early '80s, the advent of television, primarily ESPN, are the best changes we've had. The two times I've been really stressed out at races were when we went live on CBS for the

1979 Daytona 500 with the whole world watching and when $1 million was on the line in 1985 with Bill Elliott at Darlington."

Metcalfe's recurring nightmare never materialized, however.

"I've always been afraid I'd show up in say, Pocono, Pennsylvania, and there's not a soul around, and I was supposed to be in Michigan," he says. "Since we've grown throughout the United States, there's a lot more travel. I love sightseeing, but I've been to so many tracks that it seems I've seen everything."

Travel was just one reason Metcalfe was frequently away from home.

"We had two kids, and we hold a record: They were both born in 1957, but they're not twins," he says. "They were born nine months and 19 days apart. If you asked my wife, she'd say, 'You were never here to raise the kids.' I had a lot of civic and community activities. I'm a retired lieutenant colonel in the U.S. Air Force Reserve, so all this time, I was in the Reserves. All that took a toll, but I found quality time for them."

He also prides himself in finding quality Japanese or Italian restaurants in Winston Cup cities.

"Sometimes I take my crew out for dinner—someplace other than a chain," he says. "If ol' Dad is sponsoring a meal, ol' Dad picks the restaurant. For lunch at the NASCAR trailer, we may have hamburgers, chicken, pork chops, hot dogs. We have a trailer that has a full-fledged kitchen. One of our truck drivers does the cooking. Race day, I usually have a meeting at 5:45 or 6:45 in the morning at the trailer. I don't do breakfast. That gives me an extra 40 minutes of sleep, and I don't care for night races, getting home at 2:30 in the morning."

Metcalfe makes no secret of his admiration for NASCAR's first family. "Big Bill was a visionary," he says. "Financially, his wife, Anne, kept him in tow. She was a taskmaster. And I admire Bill Jr.'s enthusiasm with International Speedway Corporation and NASCAR through all the turmoil and controversies."

Metcalfe realized in 1998 that his enthusiasm was waning.

"We worked something like 17 straight weeks," he says. "Then I went to the banquet in New York, spent a week and a half on my annual scoring report, went to Daytona and presented it, came home for nine days over Christmas, back to Daytona for testing for three weeks, home for two days, took the scoring and timing equipment to Long Island to get it repaired, came home for two days, then on to Daytona. It was very difficult.

"Frankly, I'm looking forward to retirement. Tim Hudson'll take over. Obviously, I've made a contribution, or they wouldn't have kept me. I'm happy I can say to myself, the France family, and NASCAR, 'I've served you well, and it's been fun. Sayonara.' "

DENNIS MILLS
Landscape Architect, Atlanta Motor Speedway

"I love a nice landscaped area," says Dennis Mills, Atlanta Motor Speedway's landscape architect since 1993. "I can't watch a movie without saying, 'Look at that landscaping around the pool,' while everybody else is watching and listening to the people.

"Gardening is the No. 1 activity in the United States."

It's a top priority at Atlanta Motor Speedway, where President and General Manager Ed Clark has a degree in horticulture.

"It's a double-edged sword. Ed wants this to look like a top-of-the-line corporate commercial facility, and that's exactly what I want," Mills says. "So I get all the backing in the world for my tree, grass, and flower projects that I think a lot of big corporate people would overlook. It's good to have someone who knows what I'm trying to do, how hard it is, and how hard it is to maintain. On the other hand, I also hear about it if we have weeds or something's not pruned right.

"We constantly groom this place, make sure the high-profile areas—condos, clubhouse, ticket office—stay manicured. Mowing is a non-stop process. By the time we get from one side to the other, we're behind again, and that's with 15-foot mowers. You never have it all cut at once. It drives you crazy. We have miles of irrigation we constantly maintain. We do the upkeep, fertilizing, and aeration. But when you don't have Mother Nature to help, you don't have what you need."

Since he sometimes can't see a movie for the trees, Mills also may fail to notice the primary attractions at entertainment venues.

"I always notice landscaping. Disney World's the best, but it goes back to budget," he says. "When you have massive crews and money, it's easier. Ed brought pictures back from California Speedway, and it was gorgeous. There ought to be a NASCAR award for the track with the best grounds."

Mills would hope, however, the tracks aren't necessarily judged during race week.

"The weather makes it tough with March and November dates," he says. "The worst thing is to get this facility race ready—absolutely gorgeous, manicured, every curb and pole edged—

Opposite: Getting his many botanical projects to look so beautiful takes a lot of time and effort for Dennis Mills. Despite this, he has plans for additional lakes and fountains on the grounds.

and then rain. Before you know it, there's mud all over. What kills me is that race fans see this place in pretty much a dormant state. It doesn't have that nice, green look it has in spring and summer. There aren't a lot of flowers available for the winner's circle or other high-profile areas you want to dress up with a lot of color. Another problem with those dates in this climate is that we're pretty much locked into having fescue, a high-maintenance grass, in the doglegs and apron. But fescue is gorgeous."

There are additional hazards when the Winston Cup Series visits. "You get upset when rigs back over flower beds and irrigation boxes," Mills says. "I saw a concrete truck dump the chute on a nice lawn and start washing it out. I actually threw a shovel at the driver."

A race winner spinning tires on the fescue in the doglegs is another matter. "Actually, I don't mind," he says. "That's putting on a show. Let them do that little bit of damage.

"Race week, you prepare for the worst and hope for the best. A lot of times, especially when the weather's miserable, it's a miserable job. Once you're around racing, you immediately get hooked, but we don't even think about having time to watch the race. We take care of rest rooms, pick up trash, spread gravel in mud. Your digestive system takes a beating. You forget you didn't eat. It's 3 or 4 o'clock. You get a speedway burger. You're trying to run, and a hamburger's in your stomach. It's not pretty. We bring cots, extra clothes, extra food, rain gear. There've been nights we didn't go home, or there was just enough time to shower, change clothes, and come back. I try to spend time with my two teen-age girls, but you drop your personal life for those two big events a year. Your adrenalin builds to these events. Then you come back Monday, and everybody's gone. The only thing you're left with is mountains of trash"—and goals.

Below: Mills tends to one of Atlanta Motor Speedway's flower beds.

"The grounds here—the oaks, the lakes—are absolutely gorgeous. But we're not even close to where I want it," he says. "I've got plans for additional lakes and fountains. We want this to be the finest landscaping in the area. When I was growing up in Jonesboro, Indiana, my parents instilled in me that nothing good comes without hard work. I've been with this from day one as far as reconstruction of the grounds, but it's tough to get to the finished product. It'll wear you out.

"But when you have the place picture perfect, have good weather, and fans say, 'I'd love to have that in my yard,' it really gives you something to be proud of."

BOB MYERS

Veteran Journalist

Winston Cup racing has undergone sweeping changes since Bob Myers began reporting on the sport in 1960. His philosophy of journalism, however, hasn't changed.

"I've always tried to be honest, accurate, fair, objective, and build the trust of sources. The latter would be No. 1. If you don't have the trust of sources, you don't have anything if you're a sportswriter," says Myers, who covers the Winston Cup Series for *Circle Track.* "My main source of satisfaction is writing a story and having people say, 'Maybe we didn't like what you said, but you were fair and honest.'

"I got interested in racing when I came to *The Charlotte News* in 1959. Max Muhleman, our motorsports writer then, would have to be No. 1 as far as helping me in racing. He introduced me to everybody, and he's now one of the premier marketing people in the country. Charlotte wouldn't have gotten the NBA team or Panthers without him."

Muhleman wasn't alone in helping Myers build a reputation as one of the premier motorsports journalists in history or in earning his admiration.

"John Holman told me I'd never make it as a motorsports writer," Myers says. "I think John said that to make me work harder, because we were friends. [Lowe's Motor Speedway President and General Manager] Humpy Wheeler and [Speedway Motorsports Incorporated Chairman of the Board] Bruton Smith became friends as well as good sources. I admire Humpy a lot. He's really good at what he does. Bruton's smart. He used to tease me. He'd say, 'How would the speedway look with a big building in front?' Then, there'd be a big building. About everything he'd tell me, he'd do. The relationships I had with Richard Petty, David Pearson, and Junior Johnson certainly helped.

"Ralph Moody, Petty, Dale Earnhardt, Cale Yarborough, Darrell Waltrip, and Dave Marcis were fierce competitors who have been really nice and cooperative, raising this sport to the level of other professional sports. I admire a lot of people for their devotion to the sport. I think it's greater in racing than any sport. I respect Pearson and Leonard Wood, who're among my best friends, and we've lost our wives, so we can relate. David loves to joke with friends. I was doing a story on Leonard in the '70s, when Pearson was the hottest thing going. We decided to do it in Leonard's motel room. I asked Leonard, 'Do cigars bother you?' He said, 'No.' So I lit the cigar and smoked up the room. The next day at the track, I was standing with Leonard.

Pearson came up and said, 'Leonard told me he enjoyed that interview. But he couldn't stand that stinking cigar.' Leonard was so embarrassed, and you know what a nice guy he is. I didn't know he *really* had an aversion for a cigar. I never smoked another one around him."

Myers has seen both the sport and his life as a motorsports journalist change dramatically in four decades.

"The lowest point in my career was when *The Charlotte News* ceased publication in 1985," he recalls. "The paper had deteriorated to almost nothing, like a healthy body catching some disease and wasting away. *The Charlotte Observer* had a good motorsports writer, Tom Higgins, so I went to work on the sports desk. In 1990, I had a couple of deals with magazines, particularly *Circle Track*, so I took the plunge. I've cut down to two feature stories and a column a month for *Circle Track* and one story a week for McLean Marketing.

"There used to be a lot of pressure to go to races and write one or two stories every day, make the deadlines, and live in motels. The media was more of a fraternity back then. You only had a handful of guys who went to as many races—20 to 25 a year—as I did in the '60s and '70s. I think we hung together more than writers do now. One of the great motels was the former Ramada Inn in Oxford, Alabama. Everybody stayed there, and we'd gather in the lobby and talk. Petty and all of them would be there. On a couple of occasions, Marty Robbins gave an impromptu concert.

"The guys drank a lot back in those days. I had a lot of trouble with alcohol in the '70s, almost lost my job at *The Charlotte News* because of it. We all used to go to the track and drink. I was doing that, sometimes during races, and would have trouble writing. It got bad enough that I couldn't function properly. Leonard Laye, executive sports editor at *The Charlotte News* at the time, told me I was going to ruin my career. Ralph Salvino from STP would

Opposite: **Photographer Paul Melhado confers with Bob Myers at Daytona to coordinate photographs for Myers's story. Both men contribute to *Circle Track*.**

talk to me about drinking, what I was putting on the line, and that I'd better stop. So did Petty. So in 1981, I stopped. That was really hard, but that's the best thing the Good Lord has ever done for me.

"My family didn't suffer from my drinking, but I was gone all the time. My wife really raised our two sons and did a really good job. I didn't get to spend enough time with my sons, and that's my biggest regret.

"I go to 10 or 12 races now, and I'm perfectly content to go to dinner, go to the motel, read my notes I've gotten that day, then watch television. I try to find a cafeteria or Cracker Barrel. I'm a 95 percent vegetarian because I have diabetes. It's difficult to eat in the press room because they don't believe in serving healthy food at a lot of places. When you come back from a race, one of the first priorities is to wash clothes—no matter how many stories you've got to write. I even iron my shirts, but I can hardly prepare a bowl of soup. I eat lunch and dinner out practically every day when I'm home. In addition to being unable to cook, it gets me out of the house.

"The inaccessibility of drivers and racing people has changed the way I do my job," Myers

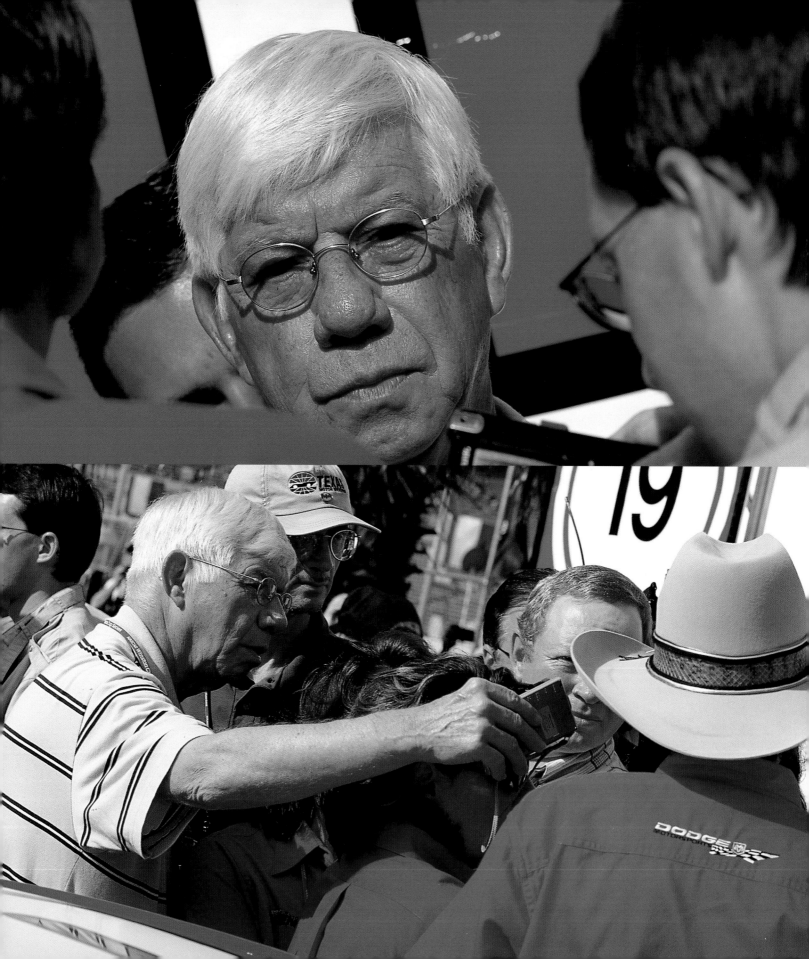

"We used to walk in the garage, and drivers would be standing around their cars. If a guy wasn't in a discussion with his crew chief, it was all right to talk to him. Guys like Petty and Johnson would hold court. You'd get really good interviews."

adds. "I try to do interviews away from the track, where a guy's more relaxed. Writing a column has become increasingly difficult because I cannot get to the people you need to get a feel for what's going on—NASCAR people, owners, crew chiefs, drivers. The drivers have so many people tugging at their shirttails that they can't get out in the garage like they used to. It's just a growing pain, but it really *is* a pain.

"We used to walk in the garage, and drivers would be standing around their cars. If a guy wasn't in a discussion with his crew chief, it was all right to talk to him. Guys like Petty and Johnson would hold court. You'd get really good interviews. Now, if you want a one-on-one interview, you've got to schedule it before you go to the track. This is really difficult, for daily newspapers particularly.

"It's almost as important now for a driver to be a good speaker and public relations person as a good racer. Drivers have to be very image conscious in order to represent sponsors. In the old days, they didn't have many sponsors. If they did, it was some oil or parts company or Joe's garage on the corner. The sport has cleaned up its image. You have the influx of Fortune 500 sponsors we never thought would be involved in racing. The number of media releases I get from companies and NASCAR about commercial deals will stun you.

Opposite top: Myers doesn't think drivers and other racing personnel are as accessible to the media today as they once were. One-on-one interviews that were easily done now require advance appointments. **Opposite bottom:** "John Holman told me I'd never make it as a motorsports writer," says Myers, who has been earning his living in that manner since 1960. Here, Myers turns his attention to Richard Petty.

"Two of the great changes were the fuel cell and inner-liner tires. Engine durability has cut the number of accidents. Tires and engines used to pop like cannon fire. You went from short tracks to superspeedways in the '60s—a drastic change. The speeds are a lot faster. You've got higher purses, greater attendance, new tracks, longer races. Television, which was non-existent when I started covering the sport, does a remarkable job, and that's one of the biggest changes.

"Nothing else, to me, can measure up to Winston Cup, and I'm talking about other sports or forms of racing. I've got a love of—kind of an addiction to—the sport that's hard to explain. You know you're writing about the best."

RICHARD PETTY
Seven-Time Winston Cup Champion

Richard Petty is motorsports royalty—universally admired, a hero to millions. And, ironically, the person stock-car racing's King most admires shares his majestic nickname.

"My dad [three-time NASCAR champion Lee Petty] was my hero as far as race drivers," Petty says. "But I always admired Arnold Palmer because of the way he handled people. The reason he had a following was he had a good personality. His deal has been similar to mine. We came along about the same time. I always admired people like that, like a Michael Jordan. He's great at what he does. But he must be good with people, because eventually it catches up with you if you're not."

In short, not only were both golf's King and King Richard embraced by their legions of fans, they graciously returned the adoration.

"When they say the King, anybody who knows anything about racing, even if they're in Oshkosh, Wisconsin, knows who you're talking about," Petty says. "It's an honor. They could call me a lot worse. My grandson calls me the cat in the hat. If my name had been Joe or Bill, they would have had to call me the Silver Fox [David Pearson's nickname] or something."

The slender figure in sunglasses and a cowboy hat set a litany of records unmatched in the annals of his sport, including 200 career victories and a single-season record 27 in 1967, before he ended his 35-year driving career after the 1992 season to devote his efforts to running Petty Enterprises.

"There's never been a record set that hasn't been broken, but 200 wins is going to be hard to break, because they don't run as many races now," Petty says. "Jeff Gordon is the first one who *looks* like he's got a chance. If I accumulated seven championships and Dale Earnhardt accumulated seven, there's no reason somebody can't get eight, nine, or 10.

"I just loved driving a race car. The only thing I ever wanted to do is be around racing. When I got to be 18, I asked Daddy about letting me drive, and he said to come back when I was 21. So when I was 21, I came back. I went to Columbia, South Carolina, and ran my first race. I told Dale [Inman] on the way home, 'I think I'm going to like this.' It started as a family affair. My brother [Maurice] built the engines. Dale's my cousin, and he wound up being the crew chief on 198 of those wins.

"When we first started, all we had for safety was a seat belt. We didn't have bucket seats, nothing to hold you in the car. You didn't have door bars. We didn't have a shoulder harness, fire extinguishers, fuel cells, drivers' uniforms."

"When we first started, all we had for safety was a seat belt. We didn't have bucket seats, nothing to hold you in the car. You had one roll bar over your head, one in front of you, and one behind you. You didn't have door bars. We didn't have a shoulder harness, fire extinguishers, bulletproof tires, fuel cells, drivers' uniforms.

"The restrictor plate is the most dangerous thing they've ever come up with. They let it get away from being a stock car. And when they did, they opened a can of worms for speed. Speed's irrelevant to racing. It's how close the competition is. We ran races at 100 miles an hour that were just as good as 200. You used to have to brutally handle a race car. It had little, narrow tires. It didn't have disk brakes, didn't have power steering. If the car didn't handle, it was tough stuff.

"There are *winners* today who physically couldn't have competed in the late '60s and early '70s. I don't care how good a shape they're in. They're not nearly as tough as a Cale Yarborough, a Bobby Allison, or a David Pearson.

"Pearson was the toughest to beat. Allison and Yarborough never gave up. If they were 10 laps behind, they were still trying to pass the car in front of them. The difference in the '60s, the '70s, the '80s, and the '90s is that, as the years progressed, the second-place man got closer

to the first-place man. You had four or five people who won races then. You've got four or five who win now. It used to be if you had a little trouble, you could still run fourth or fifth and be a lap down. You get a lap down now, you're 15th or 20th. It doesn't make it tougher to win. It's just tougher to finish well if you have trouble."

Petty Enterprises' 270 victories and 10 championships are Winston Cup records. But the last title came in 1979, and only three of those wins have come since Petty earned his 200th triumph in 1984.

"The New York Yankees came back. I don't see why we can't. But I don't know that anybody will ever be competitive for as many years as we were," Petty says. "If we weren't first, we were second or third every year, and that's from the time my father started in 1949. We let it get away from us in the late '70s or early '80s. Other people started getting more money than we got. If you had the money, you could buy the same thing Junior Johnson had or Richard Petty had or Glen Wood had. When Junior and the Woods were winning and doing their thing, they were making all their parts. They were more creative as far as making better things and making things work better.

"Being a car owner isn't nearly as much fun as driving, but the closest I can get now to driving is putting the crew together and them going out and doing the job I think they're capable of doing. A lot of times you can get talent together, but it's not a team because they're not team players. To have a good team, you cannot have each of them trying to be a hero. It's tough to get people to blend as one. That's the toughest job a car owner has.

"People think car owners have all the money they need to do what they need to do, and that's not so. There might be one or two who could keep pouring money in it, but the majority have to work on budgets. Ten years ago, you could probably operate on $2 million or $2.5 million. Now, you're looking at $8 million or $10 million per car. A little more than a third goes to payroll. My salary has always been whatever the Social Security break was. It used to be $20,000. Then it went to $50,000. Then it went to [$72,600 in 1999]. That's what I draw out of the company. I make my money on personal appearances, selling T-shirts or hats.

"It's a 24-hour-a-day business. We've got three planes. I sit in the back and sleep. I don't look forward to going to bed. I don't look forward to getting up. I don't look forward to eating. I've never been on a regular schedule. If I take a half-hour nap, I can go another 12 hours. If we have to stay up for 28 or 50 hours or whatever, I go right along with it. But if I get a chance to

"Being a car owner isn't nearly as much fun as driving, but the closest I can get now to driving is putting the crew together and them going out and doing the job I think they're capable of doing."

"Most people put on a hat and sunglasses to hide. I take mine off. But there's always somebody who recognizes you. An Earnhardt or a Gordon can't go anywhere."

sleep 12 or 14 hours, I'll do that, too. I spent a lot of time in the back of the truck sleeping. They'd have to wake me up to start the Daytona 500.

"I'm probably home at the most two days a week. I'm liable to be doing something for the Richard Petty Driving Experience, be at a Busch race, a truck race, or with [son] Kyle and John Andretti with the Winston Cup deal. Sometimes I hit two or three of those a weekend. I've still got to do appearances for sponsors. When you make an appearance, you're going in front of the fans who buy the products you're trying to sell. They're supporting you. So you have to go say thank you from time to time. I'm still as busy doing sponsor relations as I was when I drove.

"The toughest thing I ever did was trying to help raise a family. I had a good wife who realized I was doing a job and needed help, so she did a job to make my job easier. Lynda did all the work. She ran the household, looked after the money, looked after the kids. No matter where we went, the kids went with us. When you came home, you always took time for the kids. You played with them, or you went to their ball game, concert, graduation, whatever. When I go home, I tell people, 'If the building burns down, don't call me. I'll see you in the morning.' I don't have a telephone at home. I've got a phone, but it's Lynda's phone. I never answer a phone. I watch TV. I read a lot. I wander around in the woods. I collect watches, guns, and knives. I go home and escape."

In fact, home is the only place stock-car racing's King can escape his adoring public.

"I don't know any place I've ever been that I wasn't recognized," he says. "Most people put on a hat and sunglasses to hide. I take mine off. But there's always somebody who recognizes you. An Earnhardt or a Gordon can't go anywhere. The deal, to me, is that what I do is normal. It's what everybody else does that's abnormal. I probably wouldn't have been able to fit into the regular world because of my personality and upbringing. I fit into the world that was made for Richard Petty. And, to me, it's normal."

Opposite top: Petty earned a record 200 victories, but he now watches others as they aim for that perhaps unbreakable standard. Petty thinks that Jeff Gordon could have a shot at that record. **Opposite bottom:** NASCAR's King shares a laugh with Petty Enterprises drivers Kyle Petty (right) and John Andretti (back to camera) at Charlotte.

FELIX SABATES

Team Owner

"I know what it's like to be on the bottom, what it's like to be on top," says Felix Sabates, who credits his business success to being "in the right place at the right time."

"I came from money in Cuba—a chauffeur, three maids, two butlers, the chef—a wealthy family that lost everything because of Castro," says Sabates, who owns Team SABCO, a two-car Winston Cup operation. "I came to North Carolina in 1964, met my wife, and got married. I was selling cars at City Chevrolet in Charlotte and working at Kmart on weekends in the lawn and garden department. My wife worked for an insurance company in the daytime and for J.C. Penney at night and Saturdays.

"I went to work in 1967 for a wonderful gentleman who had a very small distribution business, Walter Reich, an Austrian immigrant who'd lost everything in World War II. In 1973, he offered to sell me the business, and I bought it. And I caught a lucky break—the beginning of the gas shortage. A friend in California had come up with a low-priced CB radio. I said, 'How many can you manufacture?' He said 600,000. I said, 'I can sell them all.' He said, 'We'll give you 300,000.' That's about $15 million worth. I sold them in one day. The more the shortage of gas, the more truckers used CB radios to find out where stocked gas stations were. All of a sudden, my little company that was doing $2 million a year in sales went to $30 million.

Opposite: **Felix Sabates, whose Team SABCO fields two Winston Cup cars, says his decision to try a three-car team, which he abandoned, was a "mistake."**

"In the early '80s, I got another lucky break. I was in the Hilton in Chicago talking with this guy who said, 'There's this guy who's got a new product. You should look at it.' We went to this guy's room, and he had a TV box with a piece of wire sticking out and a joy stick on top. I said, 'What is *that*?' It was a game called Pong, and I got the rights to distribute Pong in the Southeast. It became a huge success, ended up being Atari."

Sabates's Midas touch continued with Teddy Ruxpin, a "teddy bear to teach children to read. The first six months, we sold $100 million worth."

He was also on the cutting edge of distributing to retailers such success stories as Nintendo, fax machines, and Compaq computers, of which he "sold about $2.5 billion in a short period."

Sabates's latest venture is yachts in the "100-foot range. Our boats start at $10 million. My

> *"I graduated from Hard Knocks University. But I'm good with numbers. If you stick a balance sheet in front of me, I can dissect it. Give me 50 seven-digit numbers, and I can add them quicker than you can with a calculator."*

---

company has sold more in the last five years than any two companies in the world.

"I like the gamble of start-up operations. I've got great instincts. I've bailed out of a lot of bad situations. A lot of people stay, waiting for the Titanic to float again. I dropped out of school in the 10th grade. I graduated from Hard Knocks University. But I'm good with numbers. If you stick a balance sheet in front of me, I can dissect it. Give me 50 seven-digit numbers, and I can add them quicker than you can with a calculator.

"The reason I've made money is because I don't care about money. I like what money can buy, but money doesn't motivate. How much can a person have? My three kids grew up, and I was on the road. I don't want that with my six grandkids."

Yet Sabates isn't slowing down.

"I don't sleep a lot," he says. "I normally get up between 4:30 and 5. I have an office at home. I do paperwork until about 7:15, get on the phone until 9 or 10, then go to my office at Top Sales. I've got 13 companies. I've been fortunate to hire the right people. I've had the same people in management for 15, 20, 25 years until they retire. I've had a lot of business ventures that a lot of normal, prudent people wouldn't have. My wife has been a big supporter. She never said, 'Don't do it.' "

Opposite: **"The reason I've made money is because I don't care about the money,"** Sabates says.

That would include Sabates's $50,000 investment, which "probably cost me $10 million," to own one-third of a Busch Series team, his initial venture into NASCAR ownership.

"I got a call from Rick Hendrick, who had an R&D team, in 1988. He said, 'NASCAR's not too keen on me having all these teams.' He gave me a price, and I've been here ever since," Sabates says of his move from Busch Series to Winston Cup racing. "You *can* make a lot of money in racing, but the biggest misconception is that we're all making a lot of money. A few teams make a lot of money, a few make *some* money, and a whole bunch don't make any.

"Forcing track operators to raise purses has been the single most important change. We should never race anywhere for a purse of less than $3 million. The other thing that's positive is going to new venues—Kansas City, Southern California, Texas.

"The racing team frustrates me because we spend as much or more than 90 percent of the teams, and our results the last two-and-a-half years haven't been great. I spent millions out of my pocket to build a three-car operation, which was a mistake. We've rented the wind tunnel, and it's about \$225,000 [per year]. Hotel operators are gouging you. You pay \$1,600 for a set of tires. My tire bill was \$1.4 million in 1998. General Motors has cut racing budgets so far back that I get 20 percent of what I got when I had only one car 10 years ago. When you spend \$22 million a year to run two teams, it's big business.

"In my other businesses, I can fix something overnight. But this one, you can't. We've got a pretty good team. We just haven't had very good results. We have in the past. We'll do it again. I have a lot of respect for Hendrick. People forget he struggled for eight years. But Rick never gave up, just like I'm not. I don't want to be considered a quitter."

Sabates admits, however, that he enjoyed racing more from 1989-96, when Team SABCO earned six of its seven victories with Kyle Petty behind the wheel.

"The first time I met Kyle, I fell in love with the guy," Sabates says. "Kyle reads more than anybody I've ever known. I went on a trip around the world with Kyle, took the Concorde on a Coors promotion, and Kyle read four books in 32 hours—big books.

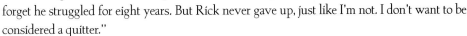

"In my other businesses, I can fix something overnight. But this one, you can't. We've got a pretty good team. We just haven't had very good results. We have in the past. We'll do it again. I don't want to be considered a quitter."

you 'X' amount of money.' That was fine with him. Kyle and I never had an argument about *anything*. I wish he'd cut the ponytail shorter, but it wouldn't be Kyle if you got him a haircut and took his earrings away.

"He eventually wanted to run Petty Enterprises. I don't know whether he made the right decision or not. He hasn't won since he left, and a big piece of what I knew as NASCAR racing left with him. It was more than a driver/owner relationship. It was a personal relationship. I don't think I'll ever replace that, because there's only one Kyle Petty. Kyle made it fun for me, fun for my wife.

"When Kyle broke his femur, compound fracture, in Talladega in 1991, I almost got out of racing. I thought, 'This isn't worth it to have a young man like that get hurt or killed.'

Another former employee, Winston Cup Series Director Gary Nelson, doesn't stir similar sentiments.

"I don't have the best relationship with Gary because I fired him. He wasn't getting along with Kyle. I gave Gary a '57 Thunderbird and paid him for three months when I fired him. Before I fired him, I called [NASCAR President] Bill France [Jr.], the person I probably admire most in racing. I said, 'You're looking for a guy to replace Dick Beaty to be a super cop. Hire Gary. He's very short of personality, because he has none, but this is a good man. He's smart, knows every trick. He'll do a very good job for NASCAR.'

"But when Gary came up with all these rules, trying to make all the cars equal, he did more to further Jeff Gordon's career than anybody. Trying to make the cars equal hasn't been good for the sport. Not everybody is Jeff Gordon. There's no question in my mind he's the best ever. Put him in a Jeep Wagoneer with three wheels, he's still going to win. When Dale Earnhardt was winning and Richard Petty was winning, there were only three or four teams that had money. Now, you've got 20 or 25."

Despite the tougher competition, Sabates isn't quite ready to throw in the towel.

"I want to be recognized as a winning car owner, like I used to be," he says. "Then, if I win the championship in a couple of years, in my acceptance speech in New York, I may say, 'Sayonara, you suckers.' "

Opposite top: **Sabates grew up in a wealthy family in Cuba "that lost everything because of Castro." His virtual rags-to-riches story after he arrived in North Carolina is the stuff of the American dream.** Opposite bottom: **Driver Sterling Marlin talks with Sabates in the garage during a practice session for the 1998 Daytona 500.**

But Sabates's hope of finding another relationship as satisfying as the one he had with Kyle probably ended on May 12, 2000, when Kyle's son, Adam, was killed in New Hampshire while practicing for a Busch Series race.

"I gave Adam his first race car, a Legends car," Sabates says. "I always said, 'Adam, someday when you become successful, you drive for me.' When I saw him at the track, I'd say, 'Adam, remember, you drive for me someday.' "

Bob Tracey

Hauler Driver, Penske Racing South

Bob Tracey, who drives the Penske Racing South hauler, thinks fans believe he "basically comes in when it's time to drive the truck, then goes home when the race is over."

Nothing could be further from the truth.

"I don't think they realize you work at the shop all week, then drive to the track, work at the track all weekend, then drive home," Tracey says. "I don't think there's a person here who puts in fewer than 70 or 80 hours a week. People say, 'You're working this many hours and now you're driving? There's no way you can do it.'

"Our race days start at 6 in the morning, so you're up about 5. So by 5 or 6 at night, you've already had a pretty long day. Then you've got to drive back to the shop. It's always hurry up and get back. The shop wants the cars back as soon as possible to go through debriefing. Everybody wants to get their job done—motors off, gears off, get it all turned around. And when it's time to leave to go to a race track, you always have to wait until the last minute to leave. We get home, unload, then start loading to go to the next race."

On most sojourns, such as the 54-hour trip from the Mooresville, N.C., shop to Sonoma, Calif., there is no time for Tracey—nicknamed "Zippy" because he's "always running around, always busy, kind of hyper"—to stop and smell the roses.

"You load the refrigerator in the truck, and if you've got time to stop at a truck stop and grab something quick, you do that. Anything quick—the lunch-break special, cheeseburgers, whatever they've got, a lot of junk food," he says. "You get something to eat, get fueled up, and go. Safety is big at Penske, so they send somebody with me on a long trip."

Yet Tracey faces a constant occupational hazard when driving a rolling billboard for Rusty Wallace's Miller Lite Fords: fans who want to lengthen his hurried breaks at America's truck stops.

"Most people think this is a souvenir trailer," says Tracey, who also fuels Wallace's car on pit stops. "Everybody thinks you've got T-shirts, jackets, and hats in there and that, basically, your mission in life is to give them stuff and make them happy. That's common for all the Winston Cup hauler drivers. You give away postcards, take care of everybody you can, but

Opposite: When he isn't working at the shop or the track, Bob Tracey is usually behind the wheel of the Penske Racing South hauler, making trips as long as 54 hours each way to deliver Rusty Wallace's race car to the track or back to the shop.

you always have to remember that you have to be at the track at a certain time.

"Most truck drivers don't have free time. You drive all night and day to get somewhere. Then you come to the track and work all day. The last thing you want to do is go out and socialize. When I'm finished working at the track every day, I just want to get some sleep and be ready for the next day. I'm a hard worker, loyal to the people I work for. I'm not here to play. I'm here to do a job."

Tracey says the worst part about driving a hauler for a Winston Cup team is "being away from your family. It's hard to have a normal life, and I don't think there are too many people here who do. Everybody says race drivers make a ton of money. But a lot of them have it worse than we do—the hours and commitments they have. Rusty is pretty much gone every time you turn around, flying off to an appearance or something. I'd say he probably spends about the same—or even less—time with his family than we do.

"Running races at night helps us get home earlier. The worst change since I came to Winston Cup racing in 1996 is adding races to the schedule. I'd like to cut the schedule back a little, try to get guys home a little more. I just don't think it's going to happen.

"I've got Tuesdays off to take care of normal, day-to-day stuff like the yard and spending time with the family. I'm grateful to my wife, Valerie, because of the stuff she has to put up with. She means the world to me.

"I do this because I love racing," he adds. "My mom, who taught me a lot, died when I was 15, and I was pretty much on my own after that. I did some enduro racing and found out I didn't have enough patience to be a race driver. I wanted to work in Winston Cup racing, and people said the best way to get a job is to get on I-95 south. So I took 95 south [from Ellington, Conn.] and got a job. The money's good, but I don't always want to drive the truck. You just hope there's a light at the end of the tunnel and that it's going to turn into something else—being a Sunday-only guy or just race weekend stuff.

"One of the bonuses they get with me is I can work on the cars, drive the truck, and fuel the race car. I love pit road. I love working on the car. We've got a great bunch of guys. I think we probably have, if not the best, one of the top two or three pit crews," says Tracey, who also cites those of Jeff Gordon and Bobby Labonte. "One of the most exciting times I ever had was when we won the 1998 Bud Shootout at Daytona—my first Winston Cup win with Rusty. Winning races makes the job worthwhile."

wife, Lisa, my son, Tod, and I took the company over. It taught me a great lesson. I have good accountants and attorneys to protect me. I don't really like attorneys and accountants,

Previous pages: Tracey is the gas man for Rusty Wallace's Miller Lite Ford on race day. Tracey waits on the pit wall at Dover with crew member Tom Hoke for Wallace's arrival. Opposite: Same function, different pace. Away from pit road, refuelings are almost leisurely. Tracey adds gas to the No. 2 Ford before Rusty Wallace heads to the track for a practice session.

FRED WAGENHALS
President and CEO of Action Performance Companies, Inc.

"My overnight success," says Fred Wagenhals, President and Chief Executive Officer of Action Performance Companies, Inc.," took about 30 years.

"In the late '50s, I was a drag racer in Marion, Ohio. Al Eckers, a tool-and-die salesman from Detroit, used to call on my dad. Eckers wore $200 suits—always had a beautiful blonde on his arm. I thought, 'I want to be a salesman.' When I got out of school, he took me under his wing, treated me like his son, and taught me everything I know about marketing and sales.

"In the late '60s, I developed a jet-pump boat, almost got it to production, and ran out of money. I developed all-terrain six-wheel vehicles, snowmobiles, riding lawn mowers, the gas-powered mini-car, a go-kart with a body on it, the mechanical bull for *Urban Cowboy*, jacuzzi spas.

"I always liked racing and cars. Diecast cars had been around for 40, 50 years for kids. I couldn't understand why somebody didn't paint one black, put a 3 on the side, and a trading card with it. I was one of the founders and part of Racing Champions from '89 to '92. I remember Felix Sabates telling me in 1989, 'I'll sign this license. Don't worry about the royalty. Just give my team a case of beer.' We kid about that now. Times have changed. We grew that company from zero to $50 million in sales.

"I wanted to go the true collectible route—take a diecast car, put a lot of bells and whistles on, and make it Franklin Mint quality. I formed Action Performance in '92."

Wagenhals's company is a giant in a growing industry, handling souvenirs for "Dale Earnhardt, Jeff Gordon, Rusty Wallace, Dale Jarrett, Bobby Labonte, Tony Stewart, John Force in drag racing, Steve Kinser in sprints, Mika Hakkinen in Formula One. We've got the cream. My focus has been total motorsports—Busch, trucks, drag racing, sprint cars, dirt cars, midgets, Formula One, CART—not just Winston Cup."

Wagenhals's 30-year "overnight success" story is even more amazing considering that on September 21, 1993, he was "ousted—the worst time of my career. Two people decided they could run the company better than me. That November, the people who took over failed. My

> **Opposite:** Fred Wagenhals, President and Chief Executive Officer of Action Performance Companies, Inc., calls being chosen one of the fastest-growing companies in the country by *Business Week* "quite an honor."

"We built our company by advertising and promoting. Nobody has to have anything I make to live. They don't need a diecast car, $20 T-shirt, or hat. I tell everybody who works for me: service, service, service."

wife, Lisa, my son, Tod, and I took the company over. It taught me a great lesson. I have good accountants and attorneys to protect me. I don't really like attorneys and accountants, but they take up a big portion of my time—a portion I don't like. It turned out for the best, because success is the best revenge.

"If I was going to make this successful, I had to get the Michael Jordan of auto sports— Earnhardt," Wagenhals adds. "Neil Bonnett, who was a good friend and one of my favorite people, set up a meeting. I told them I could pay $300,000 in royalties in a year if they gave me exclusive rights on diecast. They wanted the money up front. My company was broke. I sold my house, went to Daytona in February of '94, and met Dale and Teresa on their boat. My wife handed the check over with her hand shaking.

"I built this company by good work ethics, good timing, and luck. I think my word means a lot to people. That's important. We've done it with tremendously good people, team players. We employ close to 1,000 [in his Phoenix headquarters, Charlotte, and Atlanta offices]. We have a factory in China that's a million square feet, 4,200 workers building three million diecast cars a month. The company has gone from $12 million in sales when I started it to $350 million in 1999. *Business Week* rated it the 59th hottest-growing company in the United States—quite an honor. I like business success stories—Howard Hughes in his early days, a great inventor, hard-driven entrepreneur, and Donald Trump, who did a great job of building an empire in the modern era.

Opposite: **Wagenhals and his son, Tod (left), join Dale Earnhardt in victory lane to celebrate Earnhardt's 1998 Daytona 500 victory.**

"We built our company by advertising and promoting. Nobody has to have anything I make to live. They don't need a diecast car, $20 T-shirt, or hat. I tell everybody who works for me: service, service, service. Anybody can get something made, ship it, and invoice it. How do you *sell* it? This world runs on marketing. When I had no money, I took every dime that came back in the company and advertised. You've got to promote, and we're the best at that."

didn't know what auto racing was five years ago who now love it. Going from North Wilkesboro to Dallas meant increasing $225,000 of souvenir sales to $2 million. We've got tremendous growth ahead.

"It all comes from hard work, the vision to see what was going to happen, and putting the team in place to make it happen. I'm not the smartest guy in the world, but nobody's going to outwork me. I get to work about 6 a.m. in Phoenix, start every day with a meeting at 7, and my day is 12, maybe 14 hours, long. Hardly anybody wants to go to lunch with me. I say, 'I want to go to lunch so I can talk business.' Everybody dreads that. I spend most of my day on the telephone working deals. That's what I'm good at—deals and marketing. I know what each division does every day, every month, for the quarter, and for the year. I know what my inventory is by division, my receivables, my payables, my cash in the bank. I don't go to sleep at night until somebody gets me all

that. I spend so much time working that if I wasn't happy, it'd be like prison.

"I have a young, beautiful wife and a three-year-old son. When I took the company back, I said, 'When we get to $100 million, I'll slow down.' Lately, she reminds me of that. I say, 'I meant $100 million in profit.' Lisa brought a lot of stability to my life. She does a lot of traveling with me. The business takes so much time that I'm fortunate to have a wife who understands.

"I really love the sport," he adds. "There are a lot of good people, from tire changers to crew chiefs to car owners to sponsors to drivers. My dad told me, 'A rich man gets up every day and does what he wants to do.' If a guy's digging a ditch for $5 an hour and that's what he likes, he's wealthy. And I like what I'm doing."

T. TAYLOR WARREN
Veteran Photographer

Although he has photographed automobile races at "more than 100" tracks since 1948, T. Taylor Warren won't estimate how many pictures he has taken.

"I've got a room in my house [in Florence, S.C.] that's 10 feet by 10 feet that has two walls filled with shelves of film boxes," he says. "There's an awful lot of money, sweat, and tears wrapped up in that stuff. But I was always too busy to catalog. I did a lot of traveling. In the '50s, we'd cover maybe three races a weekend, a Friday night, a Saturday night, and a Sunday afternoon."

While those boxes contain perhaps 1,000,000 photos of racing history, Warren has little trouble identifying which picture is indeed one in a million.

"The first Daytona 500 was pretty exciting," he recalls. "I was positioned along pit road, maybe 100 feet from the start/finish line, to shoot the finish. It was an angle where you'd get the front of the car, the number on the car, and what's on the track. I punched a button when they came across. Big Bill [France] was underneath the flagstand at the fence. Bill made the call that Johnny Beauchamp had won. But being that close to the cars and the speed they were going, it was very difficult to figure out.

"I processed the film and saw it was awfully close—and *not* the way it had been called. This photo was concrete proof who the winner was. Bill said, 'You're at an angle, so the cars may have changed position.' At least that was his story. The next morning, Bill was calling anybody who had film and movies. He just wanted to be sure and didn't want any more controversy. Bill was a great person. I didn't approve of some things he did, but he got the organization where it is. We waited three days. Then, after Bill got a look at all the film he could get, he made his decision."

Warren's photo proved, as NASCAR's founder announced 61 hours later, that Lee Petty had edged Beauchamp to win the 1959 Daytona 500.

"I made the picture of Lee with the trophy," Warren recalls. "He must have realized he was going to be the winner. He stayed around to collect his money."

Warren, proprietor of Pictures Incorporated, was Daytona International Speedway's official photographer when that inaugural Daytona 500 was contested.

"The cars were plain with a shoe-polish number. They didn't have six million decals. You couldn't shoot a burst of film. You had to make one shot count. Timing is important. You develop timing by experience."

"I'd wanted to be a photographer since I was in high school in Wyoming, Delaware," he says. "After I graduated from Rochester (N.Y.) Institute of Technology, I started shooting the Roaring Roadsters at Milwaukee Fair Grounds. When I went to work for a color lab in High Point (N.C.) in '51, I was sending stuff to Chris Economaki at *National Speed Sport News* and to Walter Bull at *Illustrated Speedway News*, which were about the only two national motorsports papers at the time. I went to see if [former NASCAR publicist] Houston Lawing wanted prints of the stuff I'd shot and got friendly with Houston, a super person. Houston had a lot of promotional ideas. Houston would do special stories for the local newspapers to promote an upcoming race, and I'd do special art to go with that story.

"You had to concentrate on what was going to make a news picture and what showed off the car. The cars were plain with a shoe-polish number. They didn't have six million decals, and you had to watch the race and realize when a guy was going to lose it and there'd be a wreck. You couldn't shoot a burst of film. You had to make one shot count. Timing is important. You develop timing by experience.

Opposite: **T. Taylor Warren has his battery of photography equipment at the ready on pit road at Bristol. In the days before autofocus and motordrives, timing was a critical skill that Warren mastered to get the shots he needed.**

"I used to set up posed shots with the driver around the car," he adds. "I'd show him how to pose. You're concentrating on producing art that's usable. The high-speed films of today's automatic cameras is easier for photographers. But you've still got to think about when to press that button, what the picture is going to be, how it's going to be used. I think photographers now are more concerned with how much film they can shoot.

"In the early days, I *might* have had one other person shoot the picture I shot, but mostly I was shooting stuff nobody else had. We'd have two or three, four at the most, photographers at a race. You have 200 or 300 now."

Seeing the number of photographers at Winston Cup races multiply a hundredfold isn't the only change Warren has witnessed.

"I'd ride with drivers—Bill Blair, Jimmie Lewallen, Jim Paschal—in the race car to the track and back," Warren recalls. "You prayed that if they wrecked it wasn't so serious they couldn't repair the car enough to get it back home that night.

"One time at Darlington I wasn't in position to get anything in victory lane. So after victory lane sort of calmed down, I went to [former Darlington Raceway President] Bob Colvin and said, 'I didn't get any pictures that were any good.' So they staged more pictures for me. You can't do that now.

"When I'm home, I'm working in the yard, working on negatives, prints," Warren adds. "I enjoy mechanical work, even though I'm not a mechanic. When I'm at a race, I stay at the motel and read photo magazines. You have to get up at 5:30 or 6 to get to the track because traffic gets so heavy.

"In the old days, though, you partied. The big party time was Daytona. You'd go to bars until you caught up with the party—Curtis Turner and Joe Weatherly. It would last until you got tired or they closed the bar, whichever came first. Darlington was a big party track because they closed on Sunday. Everybody would gather at a motel pool because it was Labor Day weekend and hot, and there was a big party all day long on Sunday before the race on Monday. In the early days, the drivers were accessible. You partied with them.

"Now, you can't even get close to them at the track. You can't get driver pictures like you used to. If you want something special, you have to set it up with their handlers—their P.R. people and sponsor representatives. We're a little luckier than the writers because we can stand back with a long lens and take a picture. The still photographers, and TV is just as bad, move right up on somebody's face instead of standing back 10 feet so they're not encroaching on a person. It bothers me to see people go too close to a subject. They're hurting everybody, particularly now that drivers are so conscious of people crowding them. When I was shooting for [longtime Martinsville Speedway executive] Dick Thompson, he'd tell me he wanted pictures of so and so, and I'd shoot it. Now you've got to talk to some handler.

"I still enjoy visiting with people at the track," Warren adds. "I still enjoy the photography. We have better film, more lenses, and longer lenses. Now, the tracks provide food for photographers. In the early times, some crews would have a loaf of bread and maybe some bologna. They didn't mind you having a couple slices of bread and a piece of meat. A lot of them on Sundays would bring fried chicken and potato salad. But photographers should avoid chicken, because that puts grease on your fingers and messes up your cameras."

Opposite top: Martinsville Speedway is just one of the many tracks Warren has served as the official photographer. In the early days, Warren often traveled with drivers in their race cars to and from events. Opposite bottom: For years this Grafex camera was Warren's constant companion. Together, they produced some of the most extraordinary photos in NASCAR, including the photo finish that decided the winner of the first Daytona 500.

HUMPY WHEELER

President and General Manager, Lowe's Motor Speedway

If Humpy Wheeler, President and General Manager of Lowe's Motor Speedway in Concord, N.C., is racing's most respected promoter, he'll insist his predecessors never had a chance.

"Early in my life, there was actual prejudice against me and anybody else in racing," Wheeler says. "If you were in racing, you were regarded only *slightly* above a bootlegger."

Yet his ambition never wavered.

"I lived in Belmont, six miles from the original three-quarter-mile Charlotte Speedway," he says. "As soon as I saw a race, I said, 'This is my thing.' I knew what I wanted. I raced from when I was 15 until I was 23 and found out I was one of the world's worst race drivers. When I got out of college, I operated [Gastonia's] Robinwood Speedway, [Monroe's] Starlite Speedway, and Gastonia Fairgrounds. When I was operating these tracks, I was handling advertising for Charlotte [now Lowe's] Motor Speedway. In '63, I went to work for Firestone for seven years, got involved in Indianapolis and Formula One—got my master's degree of sorts in racing. Firestone got out of racing, and I did the same until '75. Bruton [Smith] got control of the speedway, hired me, and I've been here ever since."

Under Wheeler's stewardship, Lowe's Motor Speedway became the first superspeedway with condominiums, lights, a posh speedway club, and office complex. Its 157,000 seats, 121 luxury suites, and 200 employees are a far cry from Wheeler's early days.

"We had four employees and eight suites," he recalls. "You'd think it'd be easier now, but it isn't. *Everything* has gotten more complex. The way we operated 25 years ago was primitive because the facilities were primitive.

"Bruton's very creative and has taken a lot of risks. We've had some knockdown, dragout arguments. He wanted condos, and I said, 'You're nuts. Have you lost your head?' He finally wore me down. Obviously, he was right, and I was wrong. The Legends cars, he didn't think would work. I thought they would. They did. So we've worked well together.

"I don't get as upset about things as I used to, and I enjoy watching a race come together," Wheeler adds. "If everything works well, the 6,000 people it takes to run an event like the Coca-Cola 600 and I have a great deal to be thankful for. I feel good when I see a full grandstand. I like to interrelate with fans. Before the race, I usually pick a couple and take them to watch the pre-race up close."

Although Lowe's Motor Speedway's pre-race extravaganzas usually feature military themes, Wheeler has seized the opportunity to add a special request to those shows.

"I remember one time I was watching the pre-race show in the press box, and we had something or other going on, and I overheard one of the writers, who didn't know I was standing there, say, 'What's Humpy going to have next? Dancing bears?' So I just giggled to myself, and as soon as the race was over I assigned somebody to find us some dancing bears, and we had them the next time," he recalls. "Everybody's put on earth for some reason, and it's wonderful if it's what we really like to do. Entertaining people is what I was put here to do."

Wheeler, a former Golden Gloves boxer, thinks he had an ideal background for his vocation.

"My dad was football, baseball, and basketball coach at Belmont Abbey College and didn't care a thing about racing. My mother didn't, either, but it was keeping me out of trouble, so she actually encouraged me," he says. "She liked racing a lot more than boxing. When I was boxing, I would come home, and my eyes were black because I used to lead with my head. I was brought up in a mill town and going to prep school at Belmont Abbey, a Benedictine monastery—taking the classics, learning Latin. I vacillated between both worlds—precisely what I do today. I'll be talking to Walt Smith, jackman for Steve Park and a good friend, or to friends in some mutual funds company."

While he was playing football at South Carolina, Wheeler served an apprenticeship under former Darlington publicist Russ Catlin, whom he credits for much of his promotional genius. "Russ had amazing ability to concoct ideas that got tremendous publicity. I learned a *lot*," he says. "In the early '80s, we had a tire test in July. The temperature was 98. There was a heat wave across the lower half of the United States. Terry Labonte was running, and I wanted publicity. It was so hot the car wouldn't run fast, and Terry was not the most talkative

" 'What's Humpy going to have next? Dancing bears?' So I just giggled to myself, and as soon as the race was over I assigned somebody to find us some dancing bears, and we had them the next time."

human being in the world. I thought, 'What would Russ do?' And the idea came. I ordered a 500-pound block of ice and plopped it on the start/finish line. I talked Terry into sitting on it. That's how Terry got his name, the 'Iceman.' AP picked it up, and we used to say, 'If you can make *The Sacramento Bee*, you've done something,' because that's not exactly the epicenter of racing. We got on the front sports page of *The Sacramento Bee*."

That's no longer a goal, because of what Wheeler calls one of the biggest changes he has witnessed, "acceptance of NASCAR nationally by the media. We're in places we couldn't be before—*New York Times, Washington Post.* Other good changes are first-class facilities, closer racing, and the ratings and attitude of TV networks. The *biggest* change is the affluence in NASCAR, the wealth it has created in so many people. When I started, it was very difficult to make money in racing. Even Richard Petty never made a lot until his farewell tour.

"The *biggest* problems that confront me are greed and selfishness—negotiating contracts, purchasing, dealing with people," adds Wheeler, who, as a track operator, has those responsibilities. "Even I gasp when I see ticket prices. I *wish* we could cut them in half. Track operators really are trying to keep costs down. It's hard to talk about that because people are looking at the inflation rate in the United States being a record low, yet the inflation rate in Winston Cup racing is the highest in history. The purses are the highest ever. Sanctioning fees, parking, security, and code issues have caused speedways to become astronomically expensive to run. There's a silver lining, though. The new TV contracts are going to take tremendous pressure off ticket prices."

Wheeler calls the speedway's first sellout, for the 1976 World 600, the highlight of his career. "It was the first time a woman had run in a major automobile race in the United States," he says. "There was tremendous publicity, and Janet Guthrie finished 15th. Back when only 15 percent of the crowd was female instead of today's 38 percent, women were taking cabs out here. The most embarrassing thing was that I thought we'd done everything we were supposed to do, but we ran out of water halfway through the race."

Wheeler's nadir was three spectator deaths at a 1999 Indy Racing League event—"the horror of horrors. It never gets easier anytime somebody gets killed. It makes you question what you're doing, the sport you're doing it in. You try to think, 'What can you do to avoid it happening again? What can you do to make it better?' And I do think in racing that learning from a tragic accident and then doing something about it is important. But you can *never* justify it."

Wheeler readily justifies making time for a personal life, however.

"I used to work seven days a week, and I still do a lot," he says. "But that's not what I *want*. I get mentally tired. I discipline myself to say, 'This is something I do for a living. I've got to do other things—family, health, the spiritual side of me—to balance my life.' I need to recharge

my batteries. If I don't, I become disruptive and irritable. My wife, Pat, is so calm, cool, and smart. Nothing rattles her. She has a pragmatic way of solving problems that I don't."

Pat isn't the only person one of racing's most admired figures holds in high esteem.

"Richard Petty set a tremendous example for drivers past, present, and future with his interaction with fans," Wheeler says. "Richard Childress is an example that people can start with nothing in racing and go to the top. Ken Squier brought something to broadcasting in the early days we didn't have—charisma and vast knowledge that he could translate to fans on TV so they wouldn't *wonder* what was going on. Outside of racing, my greatest non-spiritual admiration is for Winston Churchill—the man for the times. I looked up to Mother Teresa—an example of the goodness in the world. I have tremendous respect for Steven Spielberg. Not only is he creative, but he has great ability to recognize creativity and present things in a completely new way.

"The greatest mentor I have is the books I read. Someone said history repeats itself. The more you read, the more you see. I'm in New York in the early '80s and had four hours to kill, so I went to one of the greatest libraries in the world. I read about Greek and Roman games. They show a diagram of a Hippodrome, an oval, for chariot races, and the [grandstand configuration] was exactly the same as Charlotte. I read about this guy who won 400 chariot races and think, 'This is Richard Petty.' They had more liberal laws as far as what they could do—feeding Christians to lions. But the Romans had VIP suites, a special area for Caesar and his buddies, souvenirs, concessions. It almost sent

Above: Wheeler conducts a press conference to address questions about security at Lowe's Motor Speedway in October of 1999. There were concerns about the potential for a bomb threat after an unexploded bomb was discovered at a Lowe's Home Improvement Center. The race was held without incident.

cold chills up my spine, because when this speedway was built, we didn't refer to Hippodromes.

"One thousand years from now, archaeologists are going to dig into this speedway. They're going to think, 'These people are doing the same thing they were in Rome, except they've got motors in their chariots.' And they're going to pick these chicken bones up, look at the wishbones, and say, 'You know, the people were awfully small who came to these races.'"

Wood Family
Team Owners

Sixteen drivers—unsurpassed by any team in Winston Cup history—have won in automobiles owned by the Wood family of Stuart, Va. Wood-owned Ford products won 31 races in the '60s, 54 in the '70s, and nine in the '80s, but only two in the '90s—and none since Morgan Shepherd's 1993 triumph at Atlanta.

The Woods—Glen, his sons Eddie and Len, daughter Kim Hall, and younger brother Leonard—haven't relinquished hope of a return to glory.

"We still look forward to winning," Leonard says. "If you didn't think you were going to win, you'd quit. You've got to have that drive. If you work hard enough, it will hopefully turn around."

"Eddie, Len, and I would like to get back to that heyday," Kim adds. "With the addition of Elliott Sadler as our driver and Mike Beam as crew chief, we're making big changes. It'll happen."

"It's a lot harder now," Eddie says, "but we're closer than we've been in a long time."

"It was just as hard to beat the bunch that won," Leonard says of the glory days. "But now you've got 43 cars with enough money to buy a winning combination."

"They've all got good sponsors and good equipment," Kim says. "Years ago, there were only three or four cars that won. You've got that today, but you don't see them lapping the field."

Opposite: **Michael Kranefuss, who directed Ford's worldwide racing efforts before he became a team owner, talks with Leonard Wood as they sit on the pit wall at Michigan.**

When David Pearson claimed 43 victories in the '70s in the No. 21 Purolator Mercury, it wasn't unusual to see him a lap ahead of the field. "When we had Pearson, if he finished fifth, he'd hang his head in shame," Len says.

"We've had many No. 1, top-notch, unbeatable drivers," says Leonard, who understandably had his favorites. "When we got David, they said he was over the hill. But we hit a home run. Jim Clark was a great competitor, kind of like Pearson. Cale Yarborough was a great person to get along with. A. J. Foyt, if some important person was with him, it made you feel good that the first thing he wanted to do is introduce you."

The team's original driver was Glen, who captured four races. "We started out for fun," he says. "As I got older, I didn't like to go as fast on Daytona-type tracks.

"I've been asked, 'Do you get the same feeling from your car winning as when you drove?'

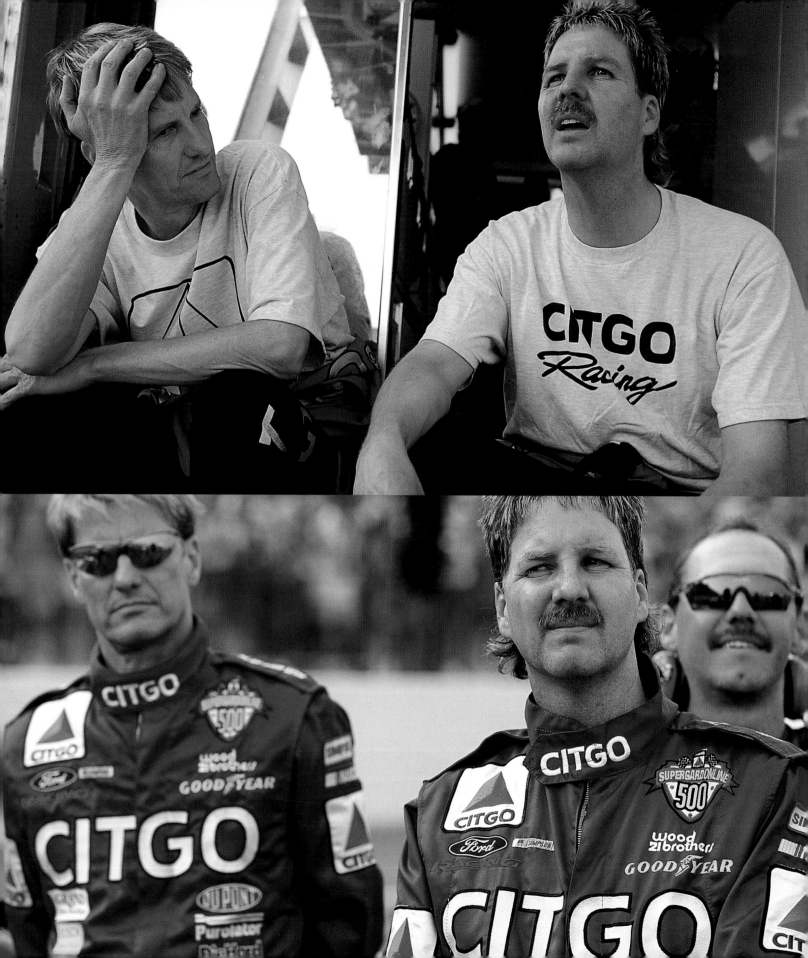

"I've been asked, 'Do you get the same feeling from your car winning as when you drove?' It's very close," says Glen Wood.

It's very close."

Kim agrees.

"Morgan's victory at Atlanta was only the fourth or fifth time I'd been in victory circle, and I *liked* it," she says. "It takes everybody here to make it work. It's truly a family deal. All the drivers we've had, Mama about adopts them. They become a big part of the family."

So does the team's sponsor.

"Citgo started with us in '85," Kim adds. "They had 2,000 outlets, and they've got 14,000 now—more than any kind of chain. That's impressive."

"We're proud to have been part of that," Glen says.

"It's the longest sponsor/team relationship going," Kim says. "We've always treated the sponsors the way we want to be treated. We tell them what we want to do, what we think we can do, what we see for the future. An open line of communication is the key."

"We want to win for them," Leonard says. "With Purolator and Citgo, it has been like family. You go eat with them. They come to your parties."

"I really respected Larry Brittain with Citgo and Paul Cameron with Purolator," Glen says. "And I admired Big Bill France, a good friend. I always thought if he could have been president, we'd have been better off. He was a leader of people."

"Bill Jr., [his children] Lesa Kennedy, and Brian France are the same caliber," Hall adds. "They're taking NASCAR to new levels."

Opposite top: **Eddie and Len Wood sit on the steps of their hauler and talk about their plans for The Winston 2000.**
Opposite bottom: **The second generation of Wood brothers line up for the national anthem before a race at Lowe's Motor Speedway in 1999.**

When the family business started in 1951, Leonard didn't envision turning his hobby into a career.

"When Glen was driving, we'd run for fun Wednesday night, Friday night, Saturday night, and Sunday. Curtis Turner and Joe Weatherly helped us get the factory deal with Ford in '56. It got so big it began to be a business. That's what life's all about—trying to do something you enjoy and make a living. I've always been interested in mechanical things. When I was seven years old, I was under the hood helping tighten cylinder head bolts. I always took pride in being able to fix something better than somebody else.

I've always admired Smokey Yunick," says Leonard, also one of motorsports' legendary mechanics. "He's a talented mechanic, extremely smart, always built extremely powerful engines, and his sense of humor is something else."

Eddie, Len, and Kim joined the family business that dominates their lives in the '70s.

"We worked at the shop after school, cleaning cars, sweeping floors," Eddie says. "It was Daddy, Leonard, Len, myself, and one or two others. As we got older, we took on more responsibility."

"The majority of waking hours, this is what we do," Kim says. "Prior to me doing what I do, Mama did it. We do things basically the same—just a lot more of it. Our payroll consisted of four or five men. Now, it's closer to 40. Back then, you didn't have 100,000 people traveling to the same place you are. My job is sort of being home base. When the track closes, this shop doesn't. Saturday night, Mike called about 11:30. He said, 'You *are* there! What are you doing?' I said, 'I'm getting so much done because the phone's not ringing.' They were in Fontana and going to Sears Point to test. I had probably 25 people going. Part of them flew into Los Angeles, part into Ontario. Part went to the race, part to the race and test, part to the test only. Coordinating that is never dull."

"Len and I spend more time at the track than at home," Eddie says. "It's abnormal being home. When we are, you've got Monday, Tuesday, and Wednesday to get ready. Hopefully, by Thursday afternoon, the truck has gone. But most of the time, it's 5 o'clock to get everything done, get on an airplane, and go to the track."

"Lunch is the only time we're together," Glen says.

"We call it dinner bucket. Mama cooks a big country lunch every day for her, Daddy, Eddie, Len, me, and my husband, Terry, who's the shop foreman," Kim says. "If one of us had to miss lunch and something comes up, they'll say, 'Where did you hear that?' We'll say, 'Dinner bucket.'"

"Dinner bucket is where we have our meetings," Len says. "We're gone all the time, though, so we try to take our wives and kids on the road as much as we can."

"First-round qualifying can determine whether you have a good or a bad Friday night," Eddie says. "If you qualify in the first round, you *might* actually clean up and go to a movie. Normally, by the time you leave the track, it's 6:30 or 7. You're too tired to do anything, or by the time you go to the motel and take a shower, you can't get in anywhere because it's race weekend."

"After Tiny Lund pulled Marvin Panch from a burning car and saved his life, he took over our car from Panch and won. That ranks with '76, when Pearson beat Petty, and winning Indianapolis," says Leonard Wood.

Three-hour waits at a restaurant during race weekend isn't the only significant change since the halcyon days.

"If they'd had pit road speeds, I would have changed tires longer instead of giving that up," Leonard says. "I preached for years to slow them down, and it has worked. I didn't want Benny Parsons pitting behind us. He'd spin sideways right into you if you didn't get out of the way. I kid him about that."

"One of the best things NASCAR did was increase the fields to 43 cars," Eddie says.

"We *love* provisionals. A lot of people have spent their lives helping this sport grow, so maybe it should be harder [for newcomers]," Len says, noting one effect of those rules.

Two of the Woods' 96 Winston Cup victories stand out—as does a 97th, when they captured the 1965 Indianapolis 500 with Clark behind the wheel in their only venture into open-wheel racing.

"Pearson beating Petty at Daytona in '76 was the biggest," Eddie says. "Our best friends were the whole Petty crowd. We went to movies with them, went out to eat with them."

"The Daytona 500 in '63," Leonard adds. "After Tiny Lund pulled Marvin Panch from a burning car and saved his life, he took over our car from Panch and won. That ranks with '76, when Pearson beat Petty, and winning Indianapolis."

The Woods regret that in their salad days, the most successful team never to earn a Winston Cup title never even tried.

"We didn't run all the races until 1985," Len says.

"We only ran 18 or 20 a year," Eddie adds. "Now, the championship is *the* deal, but not back then."

"Looking back, we should have run them all. Purolator would have given us enough money, but we didn't realize that," Glen says.

"When we could have won it, I regret we didn't try," Leonard says. "It would be nice to have won."

JOHN YOUK
Gas Man and Cook, Team SABCO

Richard Petty is stock-car racing's most recognizable figure. But a neophyte may have less trouble identifying Big John Youk, Team SABCO's 6-foot-6, 292-pound chef and the spitting image of a Super Bowl-winning coach turned TV analyst.

"A friend of mine said the first time he ever met me, he thought I was John Madden. A magazine said I'm a cross between Leonid Brezhnev and Madden," Youk says.

During races, Youk handles the second can of gas for Sterling Marlin's Chevrolet, but his most visible duty is fueling the crew.

"When they're hungry, their mind isn't on work," Youk says. "The guys were tired of lunch meat and peanut butter. I said, 'Get a grill. I'll cook.' I love cooking in the kitchen, but grilling is fun. At home, you've got a beer on the side. You're grilling and chilling.

"I love food. I pick the menus, try to mix it up. Yesterday, our engine builder said, 'That's the best ham and cheese sandwich I've ever had.' My fiance owns a delicatessen. When we go to Dover, we'll prepare cheesesteaks at the deli. I'll heat everything on the grill—mushrooms, onions, peppers. They love the Sloppy Joe's, my recipe, which I prepared on *Peachtree Morning*, a TV show in Atlanta. I did a TV show in Birmingham, where I cooked a chicken the crew just shovels into their heads. They'd eat their fingers if they weren't attached. It makes me wonder if they eat at home."

Youk became interested in racing in the early '70s, when he'd "listen to races on the radio and say, 'I've got to see one of these.' I got to go to Pocono in '74. The next thing you know, I've got to go one step further."

A trip to Pocono in June of 1979 led to a brief stint with Jimmy Means's team in which Big John spent most of his time "standing around, which I didn't want to do."

"James Hylton said, 'I'll put you to work.' The first time I jacked the car for James, smoke billowed off those brakes. I said, 'What if he has brake failure? He's coming in like a bowling ball, and we're junk.' One of the best changes is pit road speeds. They've saved a lot of life and limb."

Youk's most frightening moment, however, didn't happen during a pit stop.

"Once at North Wilkesboro, I had to run to get gas," he says. "I'm racing back to the pits, and the rear wheel of the gas wagon hit somebody's stop sign handle. It tipped over, and 11 gallons of fuel was spraying everywhere. One change I want to see—but it falls on deaf ears—is those gas carts need a fire extinguisher, dry chemical, or whatever it takes to snuff gasoline fire. You're going to have a problem."

Youk joined his current team when Hylton unexpectedly didn't show up for a Pocono race in 1986.

"Gary Nelson's jackman was hurt," he recalls. "I walked up to Gary [a former crew chief who is now the Winston Cup Series Director] and said, 'You got a minute?' He said, 'Who's asking?' I said, 'I'm Big John, formerly, I guess, from James Hylton's crew.' He said, 'What do you mean formerly?' I said, 'He was supposed to show up this weekend and didn't. I understand you might need a jackman.' He said, 'I don't need a jackman. Have you ever gassed a car?' I said, 'I've helped gas the car, done the jack, all that.' He said, 'I may need you to hand the second can of gas. How much is it going to cost? I don't appreciate free help.' I'd been a volunteer for James for six-and-a-half years. Payment was he'd take us to dinner. I said, 'Pay me what you see my capabilities are.' Gary said, 'You've got a deal.'

"I couldn't believe I was on a team that had just won the Daytona 500 with Geoff Bodine. I went from rags to riches. James was always low budget, and here's a Rick Hendrick team in the top five in points. Felix [Sabates] purchased the team after the 1988 season, and I came with it."

Although Big John often flies from his home in Chalpont, Pa., to the races, that isn't his preference.

"The ones within striking distance, I love to get in the truck and drive," he says. "To come down Virginia on Interstate-81 is a beautiful ride—awesome.

"Race day's the biggest crush you've ever seen. If the track opens at 7, you get up at 5. I have to get lunch ready, clean up, put on the uniform, and be there for the national anthem. On pit stops, I hand the second can of gas to Jerry Schweitz. It's 84 pounds—not for a small person to handle. We're a pretty good fuel team. After the race, it takes half an hour to get the hauler loaded. I get in my truck. If it's Darlington and I'm on the road by 5:30, I'm in the door at 2:30 a.m."

Youk's fiance is "pretty tolerant" about his passion for racing, which often includes leaving early for a race to "smell the roses."

Opposite: After the crew's complaints about food at the track, Team SABCO bought a grill, and Youk volunteered to cook. Chicken and sausage are among the popular menu items he prepares, and venison is often offered during hunting season.

"You can't just go to the hotel or bar all the time," he says. "That's wasting time. You've got to go outside. There are things to see, like when you're out West, the mountains—awesome.

"When I get home, it's awesome," he adds. "I'm a carpenter, and I ran a successful body shop for more than 20 years. My dad flew 31 missions in World War II, taught me how to become a man, how to be a carpenter, how to hunt. I love deer hunting, the outdoors, the

woods, the quiet. I got nine last year. I hunt other states and pick up roadkill bucks. I love deer meat and hate to see them go to waste. I also love gardening, flower beds. A neighbor told a friend of ours, 'I have somebody do my lawn twice a month. John does his own. He's not home that much, and it looks like a country club.' If I'm able to make it look that good, it's an inspiration for them to do it."

With such an "awesome" home life, why keep returning to the races?

Above: Youk thinks NASCAR should require fire extinguishers on the carts used to haul gas cans at races. Youk waits at the gas pumps at Michigan.

"I want to win," he says. "I've got that drive. The best moment was winning Pocono with Kyle Petty in 1993—being a winner at home. And for years, I was watching everybody in victory lane at Daytona, wondering what that's like. When I got there, when Sterling won a 125-miler in 1998, I couldn't control my emotions. I cried like a baby. It was awesome."

ACKNOWLEDGMENTS

This book wouldn't exist without the assistance of many people who lead *Stock-Car Racing Lives.*

For their help in arranging interviews, I'd like to thank Martha Jane Bonkemeyer of Petty Enterprises; Doug Cox of Cox Marketing; Meri Beth Garland of Action Sports Image, LLC; Wanda Goddard of Lowe's Motor Speedway; Billy Jones of Buckshot Racing; Amanda Keaton of Bill Elliott Racing; Josh Neelon of Bobby Labonte Enterprises; Tom Roberts of Tom Roberts Public Relations; Susan Russo of Sam Bass Illustration & Design, Inc.; Jon Sands of Tyler Jet Motorsports; and Tim Sullivan and Jimmy White of Camp & Associates.

I offer my deepest appreciation to Jerry Gappens of Lowe's Motor Speedway and Rick Humphrey of Talladega Superspeedway for rolling out the red carpet and to Ed Clark of Atlanta Motor Speedway for answering so many questions about behind-the-scenes racing personalities from the past.

My undying gratitude and appreciation goes to those who were interviewed for the book: Jay Adamczyk, Sam Bass, Tim Bertoni, Brett Bodine, David Carmichael, Bill Connell, Ray Cooper, Renee Cope, Jimmy Cox, Bill Elliott, Benny Ertel, Myra Faulkenbury, Eli Gold, Frances Goss, Kim Hall, Max Helton, Jane Hogan, Dan Hughes, Ned Jarrett, Buckshot Jones, Hank Jones, Dean Kessel, Bobby Labonte, Juliet Macur, Larry McReynolds, Morris Metcalfe, Dennis Mills, Bob Myers, Richard Petty, Felix Sabates, Bob Tracey, Fred Wagenhals, T. Taylor Warren, Humpy Wheeler, Eddie Wood, Glen Wood, Len Wood, Leonard Wood, and John Youk. *Stock-Car Racing Lives* could not have been written without your gracious gifts of time, cooperation, and candor. Special thanks go to Bodine, Ertel, Goss, Tracey, Wagenhals, and Warren who, through no fault of their own, endured the interview process twice.

My deepest thanks goes to Valerie for her love, encouragement, and support.

Finally, I'd like to salute:

— Tom Morgan and Liz McGhee for their terrific design of the book;

— Nigel Kinrade, whose world-class photography so wonderfully illustrates this book;

— David Bull, for giving me the opportunity to write *Stock-Car Racing Lives*;

— And, most significantly, Skylar Browning, who so ably directed this project—his brainchild—for David Bull Publishing.

— RICHARD SOWERS

Following page: **Photographer Nigel Kinrade and author Richard Sowers (right) take a moment off from working on *Stock-Car Racing Lives* in the garage area at Talladega Superspeedway. (Photo by Kevin Thorne)**